The Murder of

Maynooth Studies in Local History

SERIES EDITOR   Raymond Gillespie

This is one of six titles to be published in the Maynooth Studies in Local History series in 2002. The first forty titles were published by Irish Academic Press; the next volumes in the series are being published by Four Courts Press. The publication of this series is a reflection of the continued growth of interest in local and regional history within Ireland in recent years. That interest has manifested itself in diverse ways, including new research about the problems of local and regional societies in the past. These short books seek to make a contribution to that research. As in previous years most are drawn from theses completed as part of the MA in local history at NUI Maynooth.

The new studies published this year are concerned, as their predecessors have been, with the problem of how groups of people within relatively well-defined geographical contexts tried to resolve the problems presented by daily life in the past. Sometimes the areas studied may correspond to administrative units, sometimes not. One local society dealt with this year, Rossin, was an 'unofficial place', known as a distinct community only by those who lived there rather than by administrators. Even such unofficial places had problems in daily life. In some cases those problems had dramatic outcomes. Family jealousies over land and marriage could lead to murder. Elsewhere family networks shaped political actions during the land war. Although local historians are fascinated by the unusual and the violent the daily activities of ordinary life are equally important. The commonplace routines of making a living in an industrial town, worshipping at the local holy well in the way determined by local custom or in the parish church surrounded by one's neighbours are part of the story of the evolution of local societies and all are dealt with in this group of studies.

Taken together these new titles demonstrate yet again, if demonstration is still required, the vibrancy and diversity of the local societies which make up Ireland's past. In presenting this diversity to the modern world they also reveal the challenges which await other local historians to take up the stories of their own areas. In doing so they contribute to the lively discipline that local history has become in recent years.

Maynooth Studies in Local History: Number 46

The Murder of Conell Boyle,
County Donegal, 1898

Frank Sweeney

FOUR COURTS PRESS

Set in 10pt on 12pt Bembo by
Carrigboy Typesetting Services, County Cork for
FOUR COURTS PRESS LTD
Fumbally Lane, Dublin 8, Ireland
e-mail: info@four-courts-press.ie
http://www.four-courts-press.ie
and in North America for
FOUR COURTS PRESS
c/o ISBS, 5824 N.E. Hassalo Street, Portland, OR 97213.

ISBN 1–85182–707–2

Printed in Ireland by
Brunswick Press, Dublin

Contents

FIGURES

Acknowledgements

I am pleased to acknowledge my debt to the following for their help during the research and writing of this study: To Professor R.V. Comerford and the teaching staff of the Department of Modern History, NUI, Maynooth. To Dr Raymond Gillespie, a special thanks for his direction, advice and guidance throughout. To the staff of the following institutions who were always helpful, patient and courteous: John Paul II Library, NUI, Maynooth; National Library of Ireland; National Archives, Dublin; Central Library, Letterkenny; Redemptorist Order Archives, Esker, Co. Galway; General Register Office, Dublin. To my own family members for their interest, suggestions and encouragement. To my wife, Celia, for her time, support and help throughout. I acknowledge the support of my colleagues in the 1999–2001 NUI, Maynooth MA class.

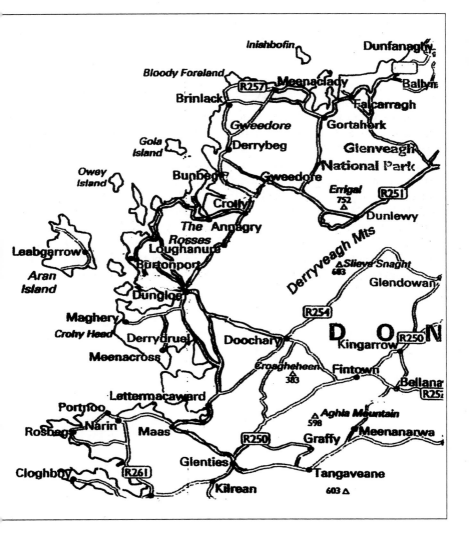

1 North-west Donegal. The Rosses lies between Lettermacaward and Crolly.

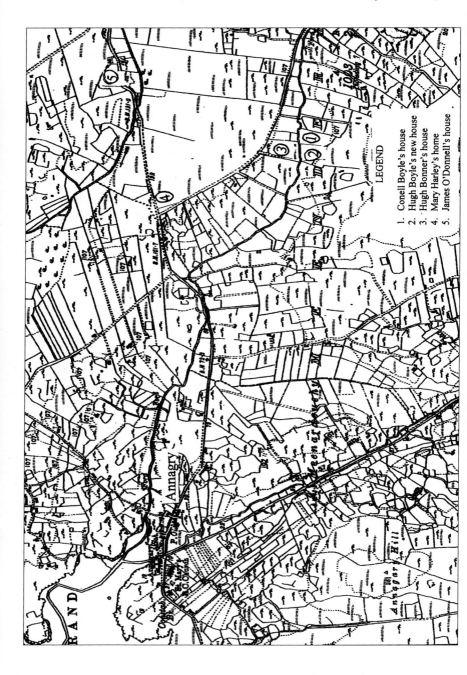

LEGEND

1. Conell Boyle's house
2. Hugh Boyle's new house
3. Hugh Bonner's house
4. Mary Harley's home
5. James O'Donnell's house

Introduction

Towards the end of the nineteenth century, the Rosses,[1] lying behind the dividing spine of the Derryveagh and Blue Stack mountain ranges of Donegal, was an isolated, remote and backward region populated mainly by Irish speakers, who revered their traditional folktales and sagas, believed in fairies, ghosts and supernatural manifestations, practised superstition, incantations and charming cures, resisted change and were embedded in the cult of manliness and masculinity.[2] The 'little farms [were] lying amongst the granite rocks, looking as if they had been pelted with enormous stones, the huge masses or boulders of granite being scattered over them in all directions. The labour being exerted by the people in reclaiming their little patches must have been enormous.'[3] In 1891 this total mainland area had a valuation of £3,796 for 11,377 people consisting of 2,226 families of which 1,863 were on holdings of less than £2 valuation, making it one of the poorest areas of Ireland with 13½d. per acre or less than 4d. per head valuation.[4] Communications were poor at the time. Without railways, piers or organized shipping, and suffering from a poorly developed road network, the Rosses was isolated from the trade and commercial centres of Derry, Letterkenny and Strabane. There was little political or land agitation, due mainly to the influence of the parish priest of Lower Templecrone,[5] Fr Walker, who was opposed to the Land League and further, to

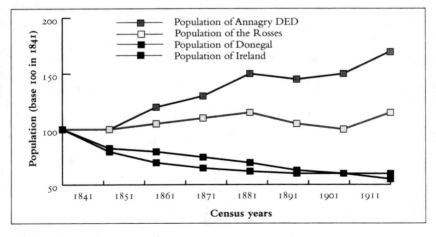

3 Indexed population trends, 1841–1911.
Source: Census of population between 1841 and 1911

9

the work of local priests who brokered agreements with the landlords, thereby
reducing rents and giving reasonable satisfaction within the community.[6]
Agitation meant drunken brawls at the Dungloe fair but there was little
serious crime. Figure 3 illustrates that while the rest of Ireland suffered more
then 40 per cent loss of population between the Famine and 1911, the Rosses
increased its population steadily throughout the same period. The population
of the Annagry District Electoral Division, situated in the north-eastern part
of the Rosses, increased in almost direct inverse proportion to the fall in the
national figures. Why? The land of the Rosses was too poor to consolidate
into larger units for pasture or ranch-style farming.

But, most important of all, the key to this population growth was the
systematic, organized, alternative economy in the shape of seasonal migration
of adults and children to Scotland and the Lagan,[7] that allowed the homes and
holdings of the Rosses to be treated only as an organizing base from which
income from external sources was controlled.[8]

This outer world was creeping inexorably throughout the Rosses during
the nineteenth century, pushing its power and influence from the town and
seaboard centres ever further inland into the mountain areas. In 1790 there
was one chapel in Dungloe to serve all of the Rosses. By 1900, six more had
been built with resident priests attached to each. This development brought
the universal church into the lives of the people and gradually imposed a
greater discipline, conformity and submission to its ways, as it fought to
replace the traditional folk beliefs, superstitions and pagan practices embedded
over long centuries. Parallel to the growth of the church was the growth of
the forces of law. At the beginning of the nineteenth century, spasmodic
military raids were made throughout the difficult terrain but as the century

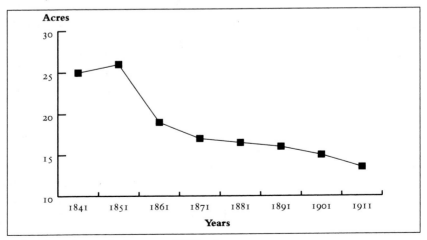

4 Land per house in Annagry DED, 1841–1911.
Source: Census of population between 1841 and 1911

passed, not alone were police barracks built to cover the whole of the Rosses but, with the opening of the Fintown railway in 1895, reinforcements could easily be brought in when problems arose. With the building of the RIC barracks in Annagry in the 1850s the sight of policemen became more common in the isolated mountain areas. In 1835 the Commissioners of Public Instruction noted five hedge schools and four day schools in all of the Rosses, of which all but one had enrolments of less than 30 pupils, and only one of which was located within the Annagry District Electoral Division area. By 1902, 19 further schools had been added, all with increased numbers and seven of these were within the Annagry area.[9] The schools brought instruction through the English language, 'when the children did not know half the time what they were saying'.[10] The 'seven gifts of the Holy Ghost'[11] and the secrets of 'simple proportion'[12] allied to constant use of corporal punishment antagonized many young Irish speakers against the imposition of the new invasive English language. Many teachers were also caught between the demands of the inspectorate to teach the official programme and their own desire to indulge in the story-telling and oral traditions of the native population.[13] The new education often received dismissive comment from the sages of the old ways.[14] Likewise, the great growth of the shopocracy throughout the Rosses where there was only one resident gentleman with the exception of the clergy and doctors in 1892.[15] The shopocracy had grown out of the local native peasantry on the back of the Indian meal and grain imports in famine times and had flourished from the earnings of the migratory workforce. They, through the clergy, exerted moral leadership in such a way that their ideological outlook came to be regarded as 'common sense'.[16] Another prong of the creeping, external invasion was provided by the poor law guardians of the Glenties Union after 1878[17] with its dispensary organization, medical doctors replacing the traditional cures, incantations and charms of the local populace and the imposition of law for those disregarding the new regulations of vaccination. On Tuesday, 20 September 1898, 18 parents were prosecuted at Dungloe petty sessions for failure to have their children vaccinated against smallpox.[18]

At the extreme of this encroaching, external world was the townland of Meendernasloe, on the edge of Annagry village, resting at the Rosses' northern border with Gweedore, and more remote, more isolated, more Irish and more traditional than most of the Rosses. Without a big house, passing trade, commercial interaction or cultural stimulation such a peasant society, as is illustrated in figure 5, was stagnant, resistant to change and embedded in tradition.

The farmers indicated in figure 3 were holders of less than five arable acres and many only had 2½ acres.[19] 'Only a major change in the pattern of life of a people, such as that caused by famine, plague, war, invasion, colonisation or mass migration, will radically effect the customs or beliefs of the rural population.'[20] None of these happened in Meendernasloe. Towards the end of the century, despite a burgeoning young population, as indicated in figure 6,

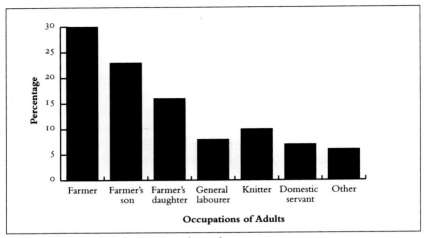

5 Occupations of adults in Meendernasloe, 1901.
Source: Census of population 1901, Annagry DED, Townland of Meendernasloe.

their world was deposited at the confluence of two cultures, the approaching pervasive, centralized state-machine with its formalities and laws, its emblems and insignia, its English language and power of enforcement, its unfamiliarity and uncertainty. This was set aggressively against the retreating local cradle of revered heritage, clan, kin and family rights and customs, oral tradition and unwritten law, justice by the enforcement of community mentality and acceptance, through loyalty, of the mores and codes of its people and their tradition. In this society it was important than none rose above one's station. Preserving one's status, dignity and name meant keeping strictly within the conventions and impositions of one's equals. Disturbing accepted practice engendered conflict with family, kin and neighbours. Unorthodoxy, intelligence and innovation were frowned upon. Nothing should occur to disturb the equilibrium of local society. But, in one Meendernasloe house, on an August evening in 1898, an event happened that shook the community. A man was murdered in his own home, apparently without cause or reason.

Nothing has ever been written about this murder and, to the present day, there is fear and reluctance to even speak about it locally. In relation to the burning to death of a woman in county Tipperary in 1895 because she was gone with the fairies, Angela Bourke stated in the epilogue to *The burning of Bridget Cleary*,[21] that 'many people were hurt and damaged by the event ... and memories are long in rural areas, so the discussion has been understandably muted'. When writing of a family of five murdered in Maamtrasna, county Galway in 1882, Jarlath Waldron, author of *Maamtrasna,* stated that 'the valley people were (and are) reluctant to talk to outsiders about the massacre, and for good reason. The event divided the valley into two hostile camps. Every inhabitant of the place was related by blood or marriage to somebody

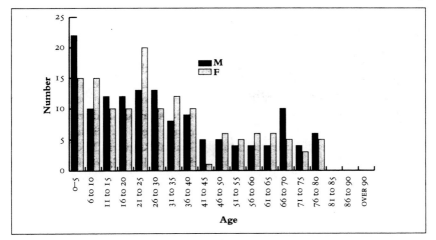

6 Meendernasloe population in age cohort, 1901.
Source: Census 1901, Annagry DED, Townland of Meendernasloe.

on one side or the other. If one wanted to live in the valley, then there was only one thing to do: "don't discuss the murder with anybody outside the family and certainly not with any stranger. It will be cast up again and there will be more bad blood." One did not even marry a person of the opposite side.'[22] Many of these same sentiments apply to this Rosses' murder and its aftermath. This short book will use that murder as the means for gaining a deeper insight and analysis of the people of the Rosses and of the townland of Meendernasloe in particular.

The narrative is constructed from a variety of sources. The contemporary Congested Districts Board Baseline Report, 'The Rosses', is an anchor for the first chapter. It is objective in its presentation and analysis and is supported by the census returns, especially those of 1881 and 1891, and I find that it agrees with the reliable sources available for the area. The three newspapers were the *Derry Journal*, which carried most news items, court cases, Catholic Church events and historical articles relating to Donegal; the *Londonderry Sentinel* carried fewer but more interesting items and letter pages that give great insight to the people and society prevailing; the *Derry Standard* is patchy and selective in its reportage of the Rosses but its succinct articles are often full of useful facts. Their reports concur with the court evidence and show no bias. The Convict Reference Files[23] relating to the Boyle case provide a firm base for the narrative. The trial transcripts are available in full and are free from comment or bias. Included are the prisoner's petitions which throw new light on the case, letters written by his wife which tell us much about her personality, official letters, prison board comments and medical reports, all of which give a comprehensive understanding of the murder, the prisoner and the background to the events. While I have received information from a great number of local oral sources, there was almost universal fear of anyone being mentioned or singled out in reference. Nobody wanted to be quoted. I have identified these sources as A, B, C, D, E, and F. Source A, who has been interested in the subject for a number of years, provided me with a tape containing this research and the story of the murder and its aftermath. I have taken a written statement which is signed by B. The statements from C, D, E and F are not signed. However, I have used these local sources sparingly and presented them to the reader as local comment. I seldom use them in primary or pivotal positions. I have used the registers in the General Register Office to establish facts about births, marriages and deaths and to establish relationships. These in conjunction with the census returns, especially those of 1901, have been useful in the re-construction and analysis of the society. The Redemptorist Order's archives[24] provide background information about the people of the parish of Lower Templecrone, their enthusiasm for missions, their drinking to excess, and their moral standards in general. These give us some insight into the religious attitudes of the people and the place of religion in their lives. Finally, the Irish Folklore Commission[25] has many records from Meendernasloe and the Rosses. They consist mainly of material recorded in 1936–7 and deal with many topics such as death, marriage, holy wells, feasts and festivals, the Famine, the Lagan and Scottish emigrations. They give a very deep insight into the thoughts and mentality of the people.

The narrative of the murder is set out in three chapters. The first chapter deals with 'The world of Conell Boyle'. This sets out the necessary context by analysing the community in which the murder took place in 1898. It examines the economic and social conditions prevailing in the townland and the internal and external influences which moulded that community. The second chapter tells the story of the murder, a shocking event in an otherwise quiet community. It was unexpected and difficult to comprehend among a peasant population who were close through intermarriage, kinship, group emigration, and the 'meitheal'[26] system but yet isolated from many aspects of the surrounding communities and influences outside of their immediate 'world'. The final chapter deals with the trial at the winter assizes in Belfast and later the 'trial' by the community at home. The differing views of each 'court' are assessed.

1. The world of Conell Boyle

About seven o'clock on Tuesday, 30 August 1898, Conell Boyle was herding his newly purchased cow on the hillside below his home in Meendernasloe.[1] He had to watch her carefully for he knew that she could calve at anytime. Meendernasloe was a reasonably steady community. There were 51 houses there in 1851[2] and 59 houses occupied out of 65 in 1901, and the population had risen from 247 to 281,[3] whereas the growing congestion of nearby Annagry is apparent, in that it had 68 houses in 1851 and 123 in 1901, while the townland population had grown from 384 to 703.[4] After the 1850s, the village of Annagry became the focal point of the community. Because of its situation at the head of the tidal estuary, boats could carry goods to the centre of the village at full tide from Lord Hill's stores at Bunbeg and from the steamers which anchored on 'Gola Roads', laden with merchandise from Glasgow, Liverpool and Derry. Only one shop was noted in the lower Rosses in 1851[5] but the village of Annagry had five grocery shops, four pubs, an RIC barracks occupied by five or six constables, a Roman Catholic church, a post office and a national school in 1901.[6]

7 Boats sailing out of Annagry around the beginning of the twentieth century.

Such advancement is indicative of the development of the cash economy within the area since the Famine years and the important role of the shopkeeper.[7]

Across the river, less than 200 yards from him, Conell could see his neighbour, Hugh Boner who was married to his sister, Mary. Both Hugh and Mary were 63 years of age, somewhat younger than himself. They had a two-room, thatch house, with walls of stone, and two windows to the front as well as a cow byre and a fowl house.[8] Their son, Paddy, and daughter Margaret, were staying with them although both were married, and their 12-year old grand-daughter, Ellen O'Donnell, spent most of her time in their home also. Margaret and Paddy could read and write but their parents could not.[9] Like many of his generation Conell could neither read nor write[10] (see fig. 8 below) and he depended on the younger Boners for handling the correspondence with his two sons, Charley and Hugh, who were then in Scotland.

The practice of seasonal migration to the Lagan and Scotland with its hiring fairs, rabbles and child labour, had its origin in the Napoleonic wars when the price of farm produce, especially grain, rose dramatically and in the momentum of the Industrial Revolution, when iron, steel, cotton, linen and woollen industries flourished. Cheap efficient labour was recruited from west Donegal into the fertile lands of east Donegal, Derry and Tyrone for the spring and harvest seasons to replace the flow of workers into the industrial centres. The Scottish farmers in the Lowlands soon became aware of this source of available and cheap labour for they had been experiencing worker shortages from the counties and shires in the north of Scotland, where Highland clearances, army recruitment and competition from the mills had decimated the traditional workforce employed in the Lowlands.[11] Each year,

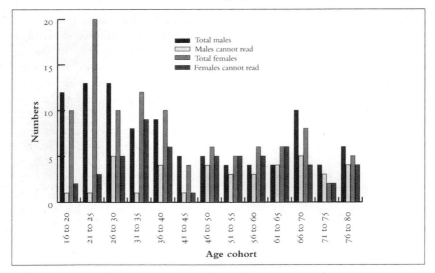

8 Those who could not read in Meedernasloe in 1901.
Source: Census of population 1901, Annagry DED, townland of Meendernasloe.

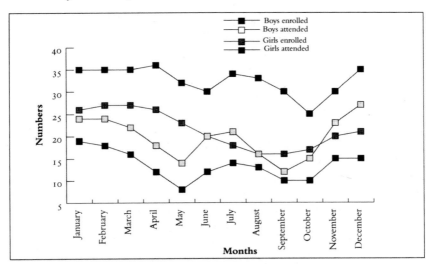

9 Belcruit N.S. enrolment and attendance numbers, 1909.

on the Thursday after 12 May, great numbers of the older boys and girls, from third class upwards departed from the classrooms and left Annagry with their bundles on their backs, containing a few skimpy items of working clothes, to walk the 40 miles to the following day's 'rabble'[12] in Letterkenny, in the hope of being hired to the Lagan (fig. 9).

Wages varied according to the usefulness of the little boy, girl or young woman from £2 to £5–10 for the half-year, and an able-bodied man could save £20 for a full season in Scotland.[13] The money brought home by the Scottish and Lagan earnings[14] was used to settle the bills for tea and sugar, Indian meal and the bags of flour and oats that had sustained the families during the hungry months. The days after their arrival home in November were spent visiting neighbours and relations, telling them about their experiences. Conell's two sons, Charley and Hugh, were on the farms in Scotland during the summer of 1898. Charley had been gone for more than a year without returning due to a disagreement between Conell and himself.[15] Hugh had gone across to work with Charley in June and both sons had been on a farm near Peebles, although Charley had headed for the borders around Kelso of late, looking for an early harvest and Conell didn't know his whereabouts at present.[16] Conell had 14 acres of a farm which he had inherited from his father, Hugh, in 1886[17] and for which he paid about £1. 5s. annual rent. Only five acres were arable so there was little living for more than himself on such a holding. His sons had little option but to emigrate.

After the migrants' return, renewed sociability on a local level revolved around dances, wakes, fairs and social gatherings. In the Rosses the young people were famed for their love of dancing.[18] 'Surees', raffles and parties were held in Annagry and Loughanure schools and in various local houses for the young people of the district during the winter and spring.[19] A fiddler was paid about 1s. 6d. and the enjoyment often went on till the break of day. People seldom ventured beyond their immediate locality to these gatherings and this is evident in their selection of spouses who were overwhelmingly local.[20]

Wakes drew large numbers because of the extended kinship in the area and the community obligation to return previous sympathies. The work of the townland ceased for the duration of the wake and funeral.[21] The body was laid out on the bed in the day room for three nights, the usual waking period to allow family and relatives to return from the Lagan and Scotland for the funeral. Bowls of tea were handed around with slices of Indian meal bread, topped with butter and jam if such were available. Tobacco was then circulated to the men who nearly all smoked pipes and to the few women who did likewise. Most women took a pinch of snuff. At midnight, the reciting of 15 decades of the rosary, followed by long prayers and litanies, was led by one of the respected elders of the area such as Simisín Rua.[22] The final prayer was traditionally for 'a good day on the day we ourselves will be going to the grave'.[23] Then, the older members of the community departed for their homes and the night was left to the younger generation who amused themselves with games such as 'Selling the Corn' which often drew the attention and damnation of the clergy because of the excesses that occurred and the scandal given.[24]

'Airneál' or 'kaleying'[25] was a normal occurrence for the older generations between Halloween and St Patrick's Day. A particular house drew crowds because of its reputation for storytelling or 'seanchas' and poetry such as Simisín Rua's home.[26] Niall Mhicí Boyle gloried in the stories of the Fianna and the Red Branch Knights, his speciality being the heroic deeds of Goll Mac Mórna.[27] Hardly a word of English was ever spoken during those sessions. Whole nights were devoted to particular topics when competitions took place to decide who could tell the best stories, but there was grave suspicion of teachers and educated people telling stories in case they might be composing or drawing from English literature rather than the uncorrupted traditional source. 'Taibhseoireacht' or ghost-storytelling was a popular choice and was guaranteed to send the audience home full of fear and trembling at night's end.[28] But in the 1890s there was a gradual falling away from the traditional storytelling to hear the newspaper reading of national and international events.[29] Conell Boyle and his dog were regular visitors to Antoin Shíle Duffy's house in Annagry where those with some English went to hear Antoin read the *Derry Journal*. Antoin normally started his reading with the advertisements on the front page in order to settle his audience and give latecomers a chance to settle before he moved to the main attractions of the Sudan, Dreyfus, or Obduman which were the serial offerings in 1898 or the many exciting scandals and court cases from Ireland and abroad. The men sat attentively, puffing their pipes and spitting profusely while Antoin, in the guise of the new 'seanchaí', interpreted and delivered the information in his own style. At the end of the evening, Conell usually went next door to Hudaí Mhicí Duffy's pub and had a drink before heading up through the village to his own house.[30]

The traditional world of storytelling about ghosts and so forth had conceded further ground to the newspapers in Meendernasloe after 1897. The overwhelming topic of conversation became the new railway[31] which would run through the townland. Two thousand people met at Crolly, on the northern edge of Meendernasloe on Thursday, 19 May 1898, and 'unanimously agreed that Léim an tSeannaigh (Crolly) should be a station'.[32] Prices would rise substantially and the cost of transportation would fall. The quarry material, especially the granite of the Rosses, would become the paving stones of the cities of England.[33] The prices of animals would also rise at the local fairs with the Lagan jobbers coming in and taking the cattle out by train.

Conell had walked to Briney's fair in Gweedore the previous day, Monday 29 August, probably because 'horned cattle in the Rosses are of a very poor, small worn-out breed'.[34] He had got the deal he wanted, a cow ready to calve, for £5. 12s.[35] Every household tried to have one milch cow at least to provide milk for the staple diet of tea, porridge and mashed potatoes as well as nourishment for children. There were 12,414 milch cows in the union of Glenties in 1898, representing 1.8 cows per holding.[36] Late August was a good time for him to buy a cow. It was easy enough to get milk from neighbours during the summer months when the grazing was plentiful, the yields were good and there was reduced demand because nearly every household had a few of its members in the Lagan or in Scotland. He would have milk for the winter and the Lagan jobbers would give him a fine cash price for the calf at the Falcarragh fair next summer.

The evenings of the fairs were for the young men and women who dressed up in their finest wear. The December fair was a big occasion in Dungloe for those who had returned from their season of migration with some money in their pockets, but the 'Summer's Fair Day' or 'The Fighting Fair'[37] on 4 June was the biggest occasion of all because it signalled the final gathering before the departure for the summer months to Scotland. The fairs became occasions for settling grievances and feuds and normally ended with fistfights among various factions.[38] This resort to violence appeared to be endemic in north-west Donegal for it was reported in 1895 that, 'in a recent address to his congregation, Father McFadden of Gweedore, condemned, in very strong terms, the fighting and drinking propensities of some of his parishioners. He said to them, "there appears to be no distress in this parish; plenty of money for drink; no need for outside aid for Gweedore; as long as this state of things continues and until there is a reformation, I will not move a peg to get anything for you." '[39] This combustible combination of drink and violence had Dr Patrick O'Donnell, bishop of Raphoe, agitated in his Lenten pastoral of 1898, 'if the fairs held in any of our villages come to have a bad name for rioting and unseemly conduct along the roads, need anyone ask the reason? It is a great pity [that] ... the inhabitants of the district could not make their markets and go home sober.'[40] So common was this resort to violence, however, that it was 'not regarded as being in any way abnormal or disgraceful'.[41] The RIC were well prepared for these altercations for 'the constabulary enforce the law strictly by arresting anybody who is at all under the influence of liquor'.[42]

It was not the Dungloe fair alone that set the local population and the RIC against each other. The people around Annagry were shocked at the treatment their neighbours across the Crolly river in Gweedore were getting from landlords, soldiers and constables and it was even worse on the Olphert estate in Cloughaneely, 15 miles away. Throughout the 1880s in Gweedore, there were constant searches, arrests, court cases and jail sentences. Then the evictions started.[43] Even the priests were being sent to prison.[44] All this time, Conell Boyle, Hugh Boner and their neighbours around Annagry could see the RIC and the Scots Greys travelling from Burtonport and Dungloe to suppress the Gweedore tenants who were agitating for rent reductions because they claimed they could not pay the demanded amounts.[45] Feelings ran so high about the abuse of their Gweedore neighbours that a boycott was organized against the RIC in the Rosses. All co-operation with them was withdrawn. When the Dungloe blacksmith, Paddy Roarty, refused to shoe their horses he was given three months in prison.[46] The carmen[47] refused to carry the RIC anywhere which meant that they had to walk the long journeys from Dungloe and Burtonport to Gweedore and Cloughaneely and back. Eighteen eighty-eight and '89 were bad years and police were being drafted in to Gweedore from all over west Donegal and from areas outside the county. The Burtonport police used to march through Annagry and Meendernasloe early on Monday mornings and return by the same route on Saturday evenings.[48]

Then, District Inspector William Martin of the RIC was killed while trying to arrest Fr James McFadden outside the Gweedore church on 3 February 1889.[49] The RIC and the Scots Greys arrested a large group of Gweedore people and marched them through Annagry on their way to Burtonport to appear before William Hammond, justice of the peace.[50] For weeks afterwards, the Annagry people witnessed the RIC bringing prisoners to be charged before Hammond. Over 400 houses were searched in Gweedore. Twenty-five people were charged with crimes relating to the death of Martin and 10 of these, including Fr McFadden were charged with his murder.[51]

The trial of the Gweedore prisoners opened in Maryborough, Queen's County, on 17 October 1889. It had been moved there by the authorities, supposedly to ensure a fair trial, in reality as much to strengthen the chances of convictions. The prosecution was led by the Irish attorney-general, Peter O'Brien, better known as 'Peter the Packer' for his skill at packing juries with members likely to bring in the desired verdict. He had Edward Carson QC as his assistant. The jury at Maryborough confirmed O'Brien's reputation. In an overwhelming Catholic county there was one Catholic, and eleven Protestants on the jury.[52] After a number of days at trial, TM Healy for the defence feared that William Coll would be hanged so a deal was struck with the prosecution which set out that if all the prisoners pleaded guilty, the death penalty would not be used and the charges against Fr McFadden would be reduced and he would not serve a prison term and the total sentences on the rest would not be over 30 years. Nineteen were sent to jail for terms ranging from 10 years to three months.[53] In Donegal there was shock and bitterness at the news for the people believed that Martin was killed in a skirmish which was unplanned and unpremeditated. One hundred and fifty-one Gweedore people, between witnesses and accused, all Irish-speakers and many without a word of English, had been brought to a strange part of the country and given a raw deal. An RIC constable had sworn that he saw William Coll strike the fatal blow, but it was said locally that Coll was not in the vicinity of the skirmish at all. Still, he was the first to be sentenced to 10 years. Faith was lost in the courts, in the RIC and in the application of justice to the ordinary people, especially if they were Irish speakers. The infamy of 'Peter the Packer' would long be remembered in Donegal.[54]

But if the great battler, McFadden, was silenced in Gweedore, the church had enough strong personalities to impose a rigorous demand on the people. For 30 years from 1849 to 1879 'The Big Priest,' Fr Daniel O'Donnell, dominated the parish of Lower Templecrone and confirmed the impression that 'the chief man in the locality is the parish priest and, except the doctor, there is very rarely any other resident who has received a good education. The influence of the priest is exceedingly great.'[55] The clergy were part of a centralized, externally focussed body more at ease with the shopocracy and business classes, educated and literate, communicating generally through the medium of English and functioning easily within the parameters of the state and its trappings of power. Their mission was to incorporate their congregations into this modern church. This was not so easy in the Rosses, especially in the Gaelic-speaking areas around Annagry where the chapel had only opened in 1895[56] and where folk religion was deeply embedded and intertwined in the everyday living of their lives. The pain suffered by the Irish-speaking population in learning the penny catechism through the medium of English in preparation for Confirmation endured in bitter memory for years after the event and imprinted a deep contrast with the ease and solace of the familiar, homely, Gaelic, traditional folk beliefs of their everyday lives.[57] Superstitions, chants, fairies, ghosts, signs, cures, curses, relics and holy wells were viewed by the clergy with disapproval and disdain, but all of these were more deeply embedded in the people's psyche than the formality of the distant, regular church. Even church occasions were often celebrated in the homes through a mixture of paganism and Catholicism.[58] On All Souls' night the front and back doors of houses were left open all night to facilitate the return of the souls, and food and drink were left out for them.

It was a night of great fear when people did not venture out after dark in case of meeting with a ghost who was seeking vengeance or was not at peace in the 'next world'.[59] The pilgrimage to St Dumhach's Well in Calhame on 15 August each year was the major event in the Annagry area. The pilgrims recited 15 decades of the Rosary at one well, then climbed the hill to another well which they circled three times, saying another rosary, while performing various chants and actions as they went.[60] The priests never attended these wells.[61] The natural reaction of the population in times of stress, uncertainty or fear of the unknown was to revert to the safety of long-held, local, traditional folk practices. There were rituals, superstitions and signs in nature for all occasions. The conditions prevailing at the time of birth were believed to seal a child's destiny in life.[62] The timing of death was similarly significant. Women washed clothes at the meeting of three waters on May Day and left them by the fire that night to dry. If a woman dreamt of a man during the night, she would marry him. Eggs would be placed in neighbours' crops to bring bad luck. People had to leave a house through the door by which they entered. When family members were going on an important journey, a fireside tongs was thrown after them on their departure. The 'droch amharc' or evil eye by which bad luck was wished on a family, a child, animals or crops, was the most feared of all in the locality. Farmers and fishermen dreaded meeting red haired women while going to fairs or to their boats.[63] Fortune - telling, by reading tea-leaves at the bottom of bowls, formed an important part of life. Some families were feared because they had the reputation of possessing the power of evil.[64] Marriage attracted many superstitions. The first to stand up after the ceremony, whether bride or groom, would live longer and a curse of sterility could be placed on the bride by an ill-disposed person who knotted a string during the ceremony.[65]

Marriage was on the minds of many parents and offspring in the New Year. With most of the eligible men and women at home for the winter there was ample opportunity to select partners and make plans. The Dungloe fair on 4 February was called 'the runaway fair' because of the number of couples who went off together.[66] More than 66 per cent of marriages in the Annagry Church district took place during the months of January, February and March before Lent intervened (fig. 10).[67]

In general, marriages were confined within the townland or its contiguous townlands, and very rarely did the people of the Annagry area go to the western half of the parish, around Burtonport. Perhaps, this was due to the language barrier or the fact that 'the spiritual state of the [Burtonport people] was very low – company keeping of a gross kind; also night dancing of the worst kind; girls dressed in male attire; running about the roads; bad sleeping arrangements, wakes ...'[68] Parents' agreement to marriage had to be satisfied. The character and family background of the spouse was an important consideration for a family. Pedigree and kinship traits were scrutinized because

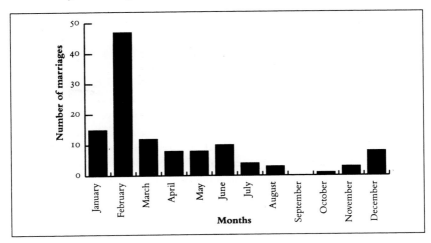

10 Marriages in Annagry, 1895–1906.
Source: General Register Office, Dublin.

old enmities between antecedents might cause some discomfort later. The
ability of the man to earn a living through manual labour was highly
important. Mental stability was a requisite. Local spouses whose pedigrees
were known were preferable.[69] The Meendernasloe community was difficult
to break into and few outsiders gained a foothold there. A comparison
between Griffith's valuation in 1851 and the census of 1901 reveals that 15
local names out of a total of 21 were present in 1851 and again in 1901. Three
external names had disappeared by 1901 but were replaced by two different
external names, both of which were obviously local women who had married
men from outside the area. There was remarkable consistency also in the
number of holdings held by the various family names.[70] Conell's daughter,
Anna, had married Patrick Rodgers of Rannyhual, a townland between
Annagry and Kincasslagh, on 24 December 1895.[71] Conell and Anna did not
have a good relationship and found it difficult to live together in the same
house.[72] Her marriage was a relief for both of them, though there may have
been some doubts about her choice of husband, for he had spent a few years
studying for the priesthood so his value in a field of turnips in Scotland might
be questionable.[73] Normally, she would have been expected to remain in the
home and act as matriarch to Conell and his two sons, Charley and Hugh,
working in the house and on the land. But their differences prevented such
arrangement. With Charley gone, it fell to Hugh to bring a woman into the
house to fill the void created by his mother's death. Hugh had to return from
Scotland in 1896 to care for Conell when he broke his leg.[74] A season's
earnings had been lost. A woman would cook and keep house, earn money
from the knitting and sale of eggs, work in the fields, and look after the men.

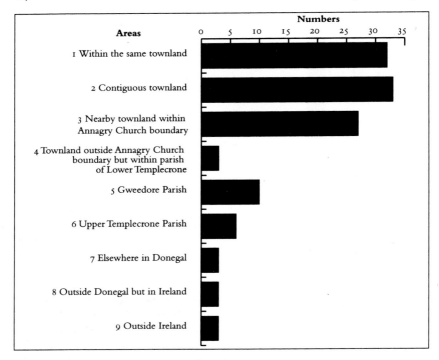

11 Where Annagry area residents found spouses, 1895–1905.
Source: Local oral sources. Author's survey.

That was the accepted custom.[75] Hugh married Mary Harley (who lived a quarter of a mile from his home) on 15 February 1898 with Paddy Boner, his first cousin, as his best man.[76] The couple had to get a dispensation because they were second cousins but this was not uncommon in the area.[77] They were both young and it had all the signs of being a love marriage, which could create problems that an older head or wiser counsel might anticipate. That Conell gave the match his blessing is indicated by the fact that he divided the arable land of the farm with Hugh.[78] Mary was local and he knew the Harleys and their pedigree. The combination would enhance both families by shared use of resources and pooled labour. Hugh would be free to earn a living during the Scottish season, and Mary would mind Conell in his old age[79] as well as run the house and work on the land.

Conell's thoughts must have often reflected on Hugh's marriage. It had only been six months since that wedding but it had not been a happy time. According to the marriage age patterns of the time Mary would be deemed too young at 20 years to get married and indeed Hugh was only a couple of years older. Mary was a fine looking girl[80] but she was headstrong and, anyway, she had the new

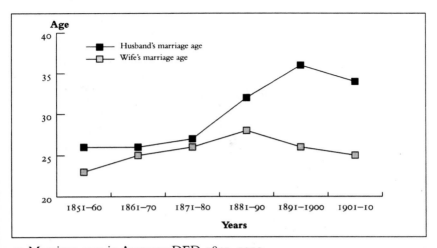

12 Marriage ages in Annagry DED, 1851–1910.
Source: Census of population, Annagry DED 1911.

ways of the people of her age.[81] He brought the young couple into his home on the side of the hill immediately after the wedding. But unhappiness resulted.

The house might have been partly to blame. It had only one room and the floor was made of clay[82] and living, cooking, eating and sleeping by all of the family had to be accommodated within that space. But at least he did not keep the animals in the room as happened in some houses,[83] for he had built a cow-byre on to the sheltered (east) side of the house for the animals. The house had to be entered through the byre door but it had served Conell, his wife and family in the old days. He could remember back over 60 years when most of the people in Meendernasloe lived in 'bothógs'[84] and lay on straw 'shakedowns' on the clay floors, eating potatoes three times a day if they were lucky, with their faces blackened from smoke and dressed only in threadbare rags.[85]

But Mary Harley and Conell could not get on together. She insisted on her own way and would take no advice.[86] There was only peace after a fight when she went up the road and stayed in her parents' house for a few days but, no sooner had she returned, than the trouble started again. Hugh and himself knew that the arrangement was not going to work. He gave Hugh the site of a house and a couple of acres of land[87] and it was agreed that Hugh would build there as soon as he could. But Conell then had a disagreement with Hugh about the stones he had quarried on his land. He should have been paid for them but he was not. He claimed he was only looking for his rights.[88] Despite some bad luck, which might have deterred most people, the house was built by June[89] and Conell was glad to see the end of Mary Harley in his own home. Hugh had set potatoes and some corn on his share of the land and, indeed, that also caused a row for he had not paid for the seed

13 Typical one-room thatched house of the late nineteenth century in Donegal.

Conell had given him. Hugh said it was a loan but Conell wanted to be paid, which he claimed was his right.[90] After three days in their new home, Hugh went away to Scotland to join his brother, Charley, at Shiplaw Farm, not far from Eddleston near Edinburgh, around 16 June. Mary went back to her parents' home and the new house was left empty. So, after having given a house site and a couple of acres of arable land to Hugh and Mary, Conell still had nobody to look after him but the Boners. The potatoes were almost ready for digging now.[91] But, after the stories he had been hearing,[92] neither Mary Harley nor any of her kin would ever dig them if he had his way.[93] They could rot in the ground.

Conell was not alone with his land problems. In all of the Glenties Union 58 per cent of the land was unproductive and only 11 per cent was cropped in 1898.[94] The arable land included fertile headlands along the coast and some sheltered river valleys, but Meendernasloe had none of these. The entire townland had a foundation of granodiorite, a coarse grained igneous rock, with bogland and marsh covering it. Every field had to be broken from the bog through tortuous toil, intense fertilizing with sea wrack and whatever cow-manure that could be got in order that it might produce the ordinary crop for the area, an acre of potatoes and a half-acre of oats.[95] The memory of such toil by ancestors of old Gaelic stock in a society which had not been planted was not easily forgotten by later generations and an insult to the land was an aspersion on a line of family. Rights were strictly guarded. Such small arable patches of green growth amid barren, mountain scrub were tempting to animals and were the cause of many disagreements. Meendernasloe also had complicated family relationships in a long-tail kin structure: for example, 12 Rodgers, eight O'Donnell, six Boyle and five McBride families[96] dominated the townland. This led to many problems about inheritance, and the natural reaction was to resort to violence to rectify perceived wrongs. On Christmas Day 1894, a vicious assault occurred on the Annagry to Crolly road at Meendernasloe. Four local men gave a severe beating to two men from the neighbourhood while coming home from mass.[97] Sarah Boyle had recently caused great excitement in the area when she threw a quantity of hot tea in a sheriff's bailiff's face occasioning him actual bodily harm.[98] Maggie O'Donnell broke 16 panes of glass in her uncle's house because he got married to a neighbour, thereby depriving Maggie of the inheritance of his house and land.[99] Lately, two of Conell's neighbours had appeared at Dungloe petty sessions. Patrick Rogers had pleaded guilty to assaulting James Rogers, his uncle, during a dispute about a patch of land with the result that the accused struck his uncle on the head with a spade.[100] A family brawl about a farm at Bedlam near Falcarragh ended in Lifford crown court.[101] Three brothers from the neighbourhood, John, James and Patrick Rogers were charged at Donegal county assizes 'for assaulting their uncle, Andrew Rogers. Patrick was sentenced to eight months and his two brothers to six months each, all with hard labour. Mr P. Gallagher, defending, said the assault took place through one of them having unfortunately taken too much drink – the old story'.[102] All of these cases were about land rights and inheritance and, indeed, some people would be willing to kill in pursuance of their rights in these matters. A letter from one of their own summed up this culture of violence, 'We once killed a man on a public road by leaving a heap of broken stones to lie in the way of his horse at night. A complaisant jury gave a colourless verdict and nobody was punished. The practice, which killed him, continues to exist. Human life is cheap with us.'[103] But yet, in spite of this resort to violence, murder in the Rosses was a rare and uncommon event as the *Londonderry Sentinel* reported on 3 September 1898 that 'not in years has a tragedy of the same kind taken place in the district'.[104] The prevailing attitude to murder is difficult to assess in such circumstances but it does appear that, while physical aggression was an accepted method of maintaining equanimity in the area, the committal of murder was regarded as a foul deed which might indicate the 'droch-dheoir' or bad blood[105] in the personality of the evildoer and his kin and would have consequences both in this world and in the next.

Tomorrow would be the last day of August. It was now eight o'clock and time for Conell to take the cow home. She could calve tonight. Margaret Forker or Ellen O'Donnell would be coming over from Hugh Boner's house with a drop of milk when their own cows were milked, and they would have his bed ready for the night.[106] He would have a bowl of tea and go to bed. It had been a long day.

2. A fearful tragedy

Hugh Boner's cow calved about three o'clock on Wednesday morning. He went to bed about four, but his wife Mary stayed up all night. Margaret Forker, his daughter, had risen about two o'clock to see how things were progressing for the birth of a calf was an important addition to household earnings. Paddy, Hugh's son, remained in bed and took no part in the night's proceedings. Ellen, Hugh's grand-daughter, had slept through the night. Margaret returned to bed shortly afterwards, probably at the behest of her mother, for she was heavily pregnant.[1]

Ellen got up about six o' clock on Wednesday morning and Paddy and Margaret arose shortly afterwards. Paddy departed for his work in Annagry at 6.45 a.m. and passed by Conell's house.[2] Ellen was then dispatched to Conell's house with milk. She entered through the open door of the cow byre and then turned to her right to gain entry to the living room. She found the inner door closed and fixed with a hasp on the outside. She removed the hasp and entered the room but, to her horror, she saw Conell lying on his back on the floor with his head towards the fire and feet towards the door. He was fully dressed. Ellen called to him but got no answer. She then felt his hand and knew that he was dead. His face was covered in blood. Ellen ran back to Boner's house as fast as she could to tell the news.[3] Mary started to scream and ran out the door followed by Ellen. Margaret followed them also, but Mary sent her back home,[4] stating that she wanted to see what was wrong with him for he had probably only fainted.[5] As well as the breaking of a traditional rule Mary would have been afraid that a shock might occasion a miscarriage. Hugh Boner was awakened immediately.

Mary felt her brother's hand and it was stiff. Then she raised his head and tried to lift him up physically but she could not. She took a pillow from the bed and put it under his head. She told Ellen to go for her parents, James O'Donnell and Nancy, who was her own daughter. She was instructed to then go to Annagry and get Paddy, the priest and the police. When Hugh arrived, he saw the newly born calf in the byre. The cow had obviously calved during the night.[6] Mary was sweeping the floor of the room and tidying it up.[7]

Before eight o'clock that morning the Boners and O'Donnells had gathered into the house together with neighbours who were both inside and outside the house.[8] Although the body had been discovered before seven o'clock that morning, Acting-Sergeant John McMacken[9] of Annagry did not receive a report of the tragedy until 9.05 a.m.,[10] even though the barracks was no more than 20 minutes away. While making allowance for any delays, there is a substantial gap in time and we must wonder why it took so long for the news to be relayed to the police. Significantly, Mary Harley, Conell's daughter–in–law, was not there though James and Nancy O'Donnell had to pass near her house on their way to Conell's home. In fact, the Harley family only casually heard of the death from a man filling a load of turf near their home later in the morning.[11] Mary's exclusion from the inner sanctum on that morning indicated that in the Boners' eyes she did not fulfil her role as wife and housekeeper sufficiently to be deserving of inclusion, especially on Mary Boner's old home soil. She had not earned the right to their kinship. It seems that Mary Harley was not above suspicion of complicity in the crime. Whatever deliberations took place among the gathering, the conspiracy of silence and non-co-operation that was the badge of later events was in operation by the time the RIC arrived. The policemen, in their uniforms and speaking English in strange accents, would not be welcome in this close, traditional community. They were outsiders representing the 'new' world and normally only came among the people to impose penalties on them through searching for dog licences, inquiring about poteen-makers, and summoning local people to the petty sessions for drinking and fighting. Like the people of Drangan, Co. Tipperary, in *The burning of Bridget Cleary*, the people of Meendernasloe 'still lived in a symbolic universe very different from the one mapped out by the RIC: centralization and uniformity had little relevance to their daily lives'.[12] And there was the memory of the Gweedore murder and the Rosses boycott.

Mary Boner was putting the ashes aside in the hearth and was about to light a fire, but the police forbade her from doing so. Acting-Sergeant McMacken found several wounds on Conell's head and face, which appeared as if it had been partially cleaned or washed. The vest and the shirt were bespattered with bloodstains. There was a pocket in the waistcoat which was partly open and there were traces of blood towards it. He found a knife, a piece of twine and a piece of paper in the pockets. Outside the house, he found about a dozen or so blood marks on the door, a large one on the right jamb and some outside the house in front of the door. Stones on the street were covered with blood in several places. A half stave of a barrel had bloodstains on it.[13] 'The house was searched but no money was found, nor was Conell's purse, although it had been the deceased's habit to carry his money about him in a cotton purse tied with a string.'[14] County Inspector Dobbyn from Letterkenny and District Inspector Bell from Dungloe were informed immediately. 'Since the discovery of the body the scene has been visited by large numbers.'[15] The police also noticed that the window of the house had been broken from the outside but there were no traces of blood on it. From this they concluded that the window had been broken to attract Conell's attention and bring him outside the house. Then the assailant or assailants hit him with the stick in a surprise attack when he opened the door. The house was ransacked and the victim's pockets were rifled and the money and, possibly, other possessions taken. Robbery was the motive. It seemed that the body 'was dragged into the house after having been knocked down, accounting for the blood marks that were found on the ground outside'.[16]

Who might have done such a deed? The shame and disgrace, which would befall the guilty person, would sully themselves, their families and their kin in the eyes of God, the priests and the people of the parish for decades to come. The consequences would be too horrible to countenance. They would never be able to regain their respectability again. As is often the immediate reaction in an insular society, outsiders were looked for in order to absolve the community. The focus of the RIC was directed towards a family of travelling tinsmiths who were less than half a mile from the scene of the crime. They had been visiting the houses of the area selling tins and cans and mending damaged or leaking vessels. Maybe they had done work for Conell and had noticed the amount of money in his possession. Their campsite on the side of the Loughanure road was searched and the occupants were brought to Annagry barracks for questioning.[17]

Constable Dickson, while on duty outside Conell's house during the day, observed that Conell's dog barked very forcefully whenever a stranger approached the house but was quite docile when neighbours or persons known to him came near.[18] This led the police to question the members of the Boner household about any noise heard during the previous night but each of them replied, 'I heard no noise.'[19] The murderer must have been known to the dog.

Dickson found a bloodstained cloth pushed deep in a drain to the front of the street. Nobody admitted seeing it so all the people present were questioned and, eventually, Mary Boner admitted, 'I saw a cloth in the "sheugh" [drain] near the house. There was blood on it. I put my foot into the sheugh and pushed down the cloth. This was after the police came. I did not show it to the police as I thought it was not worth much.'[20] Whether this was her real motive or not is arguable. It may have been part of a plan of non co-operation hatched in Conell's home earlier that morning.

Mary Harley had slept in bed with her mother, Margaret on Tuesday night.[21] Local opinion suggests that they made discrete attendance at Conell's house where the Boners were definitely the chief mourners together with Conell's daughter, Anna. Margaret Harley was definitely there[22] and her daughter Mary was probably there too, for their absence would have been interpreted as having some guilt association with the crime. Anyway, it was the custom that, even in the middle of severe feuds, neighbours buried their venom to pay respects at the bier of the dead.[23]

The next step in the conspiracy then took place. Instead of sending the telegram from the Annagry post office, a few hundred yards from her parents'

14 Gweedore Hotel. Mary Harley sent the telegrams from here.

house, Mary Harley went to the Gweedore Hotel, more than five miles distant and wired Hugh from there: 'Father found dead in the house this morning.'[24] This strange action, whether condoned by the Boners or not, was, no doubt, prompted by the fact that the Annagry post-mistress, Sophie Duffy, had been the wife of an RIC constable, John Deegan, who had broken RIC rules by marrying within five years of his entry to the force. A peeved local publican, who was aware of the secret marriage, wrote a letter to the RIC authorities informing them of Deegan's marital situation. He was transferred to Monasterevan in Co. Kildare at 24 hours' notice. He arrived there feeling very unwell and was taken to Athy Workhouse where he died without regaining consciousness.[25] The young widow remained in Annagry and continued to work alongside her mother in the post office.[26]

She had been approached by the police to confirm the passage of letters and to identify Hugh Boyle's handwriting, for the police had knowledge that a letter had come from Hugh to Conell a couple of days before his death, and this letter had to be read to him because of his illiteracy.[27] Sophie confirmed that she could identify the handwriting and furnished them with a statement of the various letters that had passed between the Boyle family members and between Hugh Boyle and Mary Harley.[28] Sophie had broken free from her social stratum and had married a professional man in uniform who spoke with a strange accent and was an RIC officer. She could no longer be one of common people nor could her loyalties be taken for granted. They feared that the telegrams would be passed on to the RIC officers. Mary again travelled to the Gweedore Hotel on Thursday and sent another telegram to Hugh at Shiplaw Farm, near Eddlestown, a few miles from Peebles, in south-central Scotland.

Back in Meendernasloe, Conell's body still lay alone on the clay floor and the police refused to let anyone inside. 'It was a strict traditional rule that, at no time during the wake, should the corpse be left alone.'[29] But the RIC did not understand the importance of these things. This made for a strange and unreal situation in the townland where death normally had an established culture and traditional sequence of events. The stopping of the clock, the washing of the body on clean straw by local women, the dressing of the corpse, the cleaning and preparation of the house for the wake, the keening and the praying should have been afoot. It was widely believed that Conell's ghost would haunt the townland in revenge for these wrongs.[30]

The wilted stalks in the potato field mirrored the death within. Set in the bristling days of spring with cherished hope and vigour, they had inadvertently become the agents of division, hatred and malice. Nobody would ever touch one of them now, for they would be tinged by the curse of the dead man[31] and no luck would come to the beneficiary of such ill-gotten gain. The stalks would die and after them, the potatoes, and the ground where they lay would remain fallow for many a long day. Everyone knew of the trouble the same potatoes caused but nobody was going to say anything. That was the business of the community and not for the police or outsiders to be told.[32]

Dr Smyth arrived at Conell's house on Thursday, 1 September, at one o'clock accompanied by Dr Robert M'Laughlin. They performed a post mortem examination of the body within the house.[33] Later that day, the inquest was held by James Boyle, solicitor, Stranorlar, coroner for the district.

Hugh Boner was the first witness and he set the tone for the rest by disclosing little information. He said that Conell and himself

> were on good terms. We did not find any money at all or a purse on the body or in the house. Conell used to carry a purse. I believe he was killed and robbed. I did not hear of him having a dispute with any person... The son's wife is living with her father now. I heard of no dispute between the son and deceased. I know nothing more about the matter than what I have stated.[34]

His daughter, Margaret Forker, said that 'she used to be back and forward to deceased's house. I did not hear of any quarrel between him and his neighbours.'[35] Ellen O'Donnell then told of her finding the body on the floor and her actions after that. Mary Boner said:

The deceased's son, Hugh, used to live with his father until he went to Scotland, but sometimes he stayed with his father-in-law. He went to Scotland over a month ago. The deceased gave his son some land after his marriage. I slept none on Tuesday night but I heard no noise. I believe my brother was killed. I don't know of his having a dispute with any person.[36]

Dr Smyth then gave a long and detailed description of each wound and its location. At the end of his account, Dr Smyth stunned the room. 'In my opinion, the injuries were caused by a light weapon or a weapon used by a weak person.'[37] A woman could have killed him. In the eyes of the locality Mary Harley's name was put on top of the list of suspects.

While the jury was finding 'that the deceased was murdered on the night of the 30th or morning of the 31st ult. by some person or persons unknown',[38] Mary Harley was on her way to the Gweedore Hotel once more to see if an answer had been received from her husband. When there was none, she sent a further telegram with the same wording as the first.[39] The police visited Mary on her return and kept in constant touch with her throughout that day and the next, asking her, among other questions, if she had made any contact with her husband or his brother in Scotland.[40] It is believed that the RIC were also monitoring the telegraph service in both Annagry and Gweedore.

While on duty at the house, a constable noticed that Paddy Boner's clothing was spattered with red spots resembling blood and, on closer inspection, his fingers and nails had similar traces. Paddy was arrested. He explained that the red stains had occurred the previous day while applying red lead to timber while building a house in Annagry village. A visit to the building site confirmed this aspect of the story.[41] Paddy was released pending further investigations.

Meanwhile the RIC had learned that Conell had always carried a watch and a tobacco tin but these were not in the house. Further information came to them that Hugh Boner might have them. District Inspector Bell 'thought there might be something in it'.[42] The police visited the Boner home. Hugh Boner swore at them and they threatened to mount a full search of the house if the watch was not handed up. Later that day Hugh gave up the watch.[43] Further discussion led to the location of the tobacco box in Boner's house also.[44] The respectability of the family was now being questioned in front of the parish.

The body was released and the Boners assumed the role of chief mourners. On Friday, 2 September, Mary Harley received a telegram from Hugh in Scotland, stating, 'starting with boat tonight'. That would mean that he would not arrive in Meendernasloe until Saturday evening and, consequently, the funeral would have to be postponed until Sunday. This incurred an exceptionally long wake with the house being occupied by sympathizers for 24 hours each day. The 'mná caointe' or keening women[45] would come daily and deliver their prayers, incantations and poetic stanzas in wailing paeans lasting perhaps for half an hour, on their knees beside the coffin.[46] However, none of the usual banter, games or rumbustious behaviour associated with normal wakes would have been appropriate in this instance. It was also the harvest season and the tradition of abstaining from work in deference to the family of the bereaved had to be maintained despite the need for the fields to be worked and the crops saved.

Hugh Boyle arrived in Meendernasloe about 7.30 on Saturday evening. He had travelled on the Derry–Glenties train as far as Fintown, then got a lift on the mail-car as far as the Wee Bridge outside Dungloe and had walked the remaining seven miles to Meendernasloe.[47] He first visited the wake house and said his prayers beside his father's coffin. After an hour or so he took his bundle and went up the road towards Barney Harley's house, his wife's home, saying that he would be back before midnight for the rosary.[48] Strangely, Hugh left the wake-house on his own which was against the long tradition of anyone being alone near a wake-house for fear of ghosts and the returning dead.[49] In a community where male bonding through the 'meitheal' system, loyalty to the group, kin support and 'deed instead of word' were its apotheoses, this casting into the darkness signalled a major breach insofar as the son of a man, murdered in his own home, was sent out into the night on his own without the support of his fellow men.

Outside Hugh Boner's house the RIC were waiting for him and they brought him down the road to D.I. Bell who was standing outside Harley's house.[50] After speaking to him, Bell let him go into Harley's house where 'he commenced to cry and do what they call "wheening" down there'. Bell took him up to the room in Harley's home and took a statement from him. Bell then went outside and considered events for a while before returning to the house and asking Hugh to come with them to Annagry barracks.[51] On arrival at the station, he was put under the custody of Constable Dickson who cautioned him as to what he might say.[52]

At 11 p.m. that night, District Inspector Bell arrested Hugh Boyle in Annagry Police Barracks on the charge of murder.

> He gave him the usual caution and he made no reply. He then searched him and found a watch and chain, two single shillings, three penny pieces, three single halfpennies and three purses. One purse contained a single Scotch pound note, three sovereigns and two half sovereigns. One purse was empty. The third purse contained a bill for £4 5s. A dirty rag was also in the pocket. He then found a pocket-knife, a box of matches, some matches and a penny, a handkerchief, a small pocket compass and a box of ointment. He examined the clothing of the prisoner and, on his inside drawers, he found bloodstains, one large one in front of the left thigh and two smaller ones there also, one spot on the left knee and one on the right knee. He said, when the blood was discovered, 'that

came off that hand,' (holding out his right hand) 'when I was going to bed one night somehow; I do not know, how I marked it.' Prisoner had a wound on the inside of the small finger of the right hand, a slight wound on the second finger of the same hand, a slight scratch under the right eye, and a small scratch on the left cheek about an inch from his mouth. When witness (Inspector Bell) was examining these scratches on his face, prisoner said, 'That was done by the fall of a tree. I have proof.'[53]

At the conclusion of the statement, Hugh told Constable Dickson, 'I am in a nice fix. It was the blood on my drawers that told all.'[54]

There was shock in the wake-house when news came that Hugh Boyle had been arrested. After all, he had been in Scotland and had been writing letters both to his wife and to his father, which letters had been read to Conell by the Boners. He had replied from Scotland to the telegram sent by his wife. And the townland knew that he was sharing a bothey near Peebles with Mickey Johnny O'Donnell from down the road.[55] So how could he have done it?

But two acts of public disassociation had taken place which had not gone unnoticed by those who read their neighbours' minds. Mary Harley had been excluded from the wake and Hugh had been sent out of the wake-house alone, not even to the home of one of his own kin but to that of his wife. Was the old Gaelic sanction of 'díbirt' or banishment starting to be applied? Maybe, the RIC were more astute than had been thought! Maybe some neighbours also knew more than they were saying!

Hugh was kept in Annagry barracks throughout Saturday night. On Sunday he was taken by sidecar to Dungloe where he was brought before Mr Gaussen RM, who formally remanded him to Derry gaol. In the course of the following week, he was joined there by his brother, Charley, who had been arrested by Inspector Bell on his arrival in Meendernaslóe, on suspicion of being involved in the crime.[56] When news of this development spread there was great confusion. The members of the Boner family undoubtedly felt relief that they were no longer at the centre of police attention but there was general incomprehension that both brothers could have been involved in the murder while working in Scotland. Nothing like it had ever happened in the Annagry area before, but the memory of the mass arrests in Gweedore, a decade earlier, spread fear in the community. Who would be next? As the week passed there were no developments apparent to the people but with rumour, counter-rumour and endless speculation, nobody was sure what was going to happen next. But at least, nobody from the locality was arrested which helped to calm fears.[57]

On Monday morning, 12 September, Hugh was taken from Derry gaol by train to Letterkenny and then to Creeslough by sidecar in the company of two policemen, a priest and a commercial traveller. Approaching Creeslough, Hugh turned to Constable M'Caughey and said, 'I suppose I am in for it,' adding immediately afterwards, 'but sure nobody saw me doing it.'[58] In Creeslough barracks, a man gave evidence that he had seen Hugh on the Glasgow boat at Derry on the night following the murder.[59] After a further 26 mile journey to Gweedore barracks Hugh came before Mr Gaussen RM, who was waiting to conduct magisterial investigations.

Two carmen from the local Gweedore Hotel, William Coll and Francis M'Ginley, identified Hugh as resembling a man they saw on the Doochary to Dungloe road on the evening of Tuesday 30 August.[60] Hugh Duffy, a carman from Dungloe who was engaged to bring the prisoner from Gweedore to Dungloe after the conclusion of the investigation at Gweedore, was then unexpectedly called. He said that on 30 August he was at Fintown railway station to catch the 1.30 p.m. train going out to Derry. On the way home between Fintown and Doochary Bridge, he overtook a man on the road and he gave him a seat on the car. When asked if the prisoner was the man, he replied, 'to the best of my knowledge he is'.[61]

After the hearing, Hugh and Acting Sergeant Kilgannon were standing together when Hugh said, 'I believe I am going to be in wi' it anyway; but they cannot hang me for it as they did not see me do it. But I might as well be hanged as banished.'[62] As he travelled by sidecar through Meendernasloe on his way to Dungloe that evening, Hugh must have wondered if he would ever see his old home and new house on the hill again, or if either hanging by the agents of government, or banishment by his own people, was to be his lot. At Dungloe barracks, next day, he was identified by two girls as resembling the man who had travelled on the train with them from Strabane to Fintown on Tuesday, 30 August. Mr Gaussen then remanded Hugh to Derry gaol and made an order that his brother, Charley, be released.

Meendernasloe suffered from an invasion of RIC for the next month, moving from house to house, asking questions, taking statements, returning to cross-check references continuously on a daily basis. Residents had to account for their movements and those of the people around them. The one singular issue being forced upon all of them was whether Hugh Boyle was spotted on his visit on 30 and 31 August. The police believed that he could not have come and gone unknown and unseen by the community. Inducements, cajolery, threats and pleadings to the variety of human frailties were applied in various degrees, day after day, in an effort to drag more witnesses onto the prosecution side. But word had percolated through the locality that nobody was to say anything. No meetings were held. Nobody initiated a campaign or set down the law but everyone understood the shorthand of the community edict and its consequences. 'Béal druidthe'[63] was the mantra in Meendernasloe to any stranger, no matter what their story. Nothing was seen and nothing was heard. The least seen or heard meant fewer awkward questions.[64]

On Monday morning, 5 October a large crowd from Meendernasloe set out for Fintown for another stage of the official enquiry by Mr Gaussen. Their apprehension was that somebody had broken the community bond and gone to the police side. As far as they knew everyone had stayed loyal but one could never be sure. Some houses had been visited almost daily and the police could not be trusted. However, there were sufficient numbers there to ensure that it would be extremely difficult for any renegade to cross the barrier.[65]

When Mr Gaussen opened proceedings in Fintown police barracks it was like a courtroom with Mr John Mackey, sessional crown solicitor, appearing for the prosecution and Mr John H. Gallagher appearing for Hugh.[66] The prosecution detailed a methodical reconstruction of Hugh Boyle's movements on Tuesday 30 August. Ellen Mulhern and Annie Smith identified him as the man who travelled with them in the carriage on the Strabane to Fintown train. When Hugh got up and queried if she was sure, Annie Smith replied, 'Yes, I am. I know your voice.'[67] Constable Devine saw Hugh come off the train wearing a dark suit. Bella M'Loone had spoken to him in her father's bar, and her sister served him with a glass of whiskey. John Doherty, a caretaker and gamekeeper to Major Hamilton, had not only seen Hugh come off the train on the Tuesday but he also had seen him travelling towards Fintown at 10.30 a.m. the following day carrying a bundle tied with a red handkerchief. Hugh's movements were traced from Strabane to Fintown station, then to the pubs in Fintown, later on the road to Doochary and then to the Wee Bridge in Dungloe. Witnesses corroborated every piece of evidence. Tension was mounting, for the case was moving inexorably towards Meendernasloe. Who would be called next? Would there be a Judas?

But the prosecution then started at Fintown station again and concentrated on Wednesday, the day following the murder. Witness after witness again traced the movements of Hugh Boyle around the station, in the pubs in Fintown, on the road between Doochary and Fintown, and passing through Doochary. Four carmen placed him at various stages between Fintown station and the Wee Bridge in Dungloe on both the Tuesday before the murder and on the Wednesday afterwards. The stationmaster at Fintown told how Hugh had arrived at Fintown station shortly after ten o'clock on the Wednesday with a fresh cut under his eye. He carried a parcel which was tied with a red handkerchief and he was very fatigued looking as if he had not slept for a couple of nights.[68] The ticket clerk told how he sat down with Hugh on the same day and they spoke about the rail fares to Derry and about Loughanure where the prisoner said he came from.[69] The mail-car driver told of meeting Hugh outside Fintown on Wednesday morning coming from the Dungloe direction and he ran downhill towards Fintown in an effort to catch the early train.[70] A publican and a caretaker had placed him at various stages on the return journey from Dungloe on the Wednesday until his departure on the Derry train with the bundle tied with the red handkerchief.[71] Hugh's movements had been well documented between Strabane and the Wee Bridge near Dungloe, seven miles from Meendernasloe, but not one step beyond the Wee Bridge had been mentioned.

When Dr Smyth and Dr M'Laughlin were called to give their evidence on the resumption, and Acting Sergeant John M'Macken from Annagry then detailed the events of the morning of the murder, it seemed as if the police trail was leading ominously towards Meendernasloe. But suddenly it was announced that the evidence was concluded. Hugh did not even make a statement. He was returned for trial at the approaching winter assizes in Belfast and was conveyed to Derry gaol.[72]

As the Meendernasloe and Annagry people walked home from Fintown, discussing the events of the inquiry, they had the satisfaction of knowing that the integrity of their world had not been breached. Despite the best efforts of the RIC, not one witness had been found that placed Hugh Boyle closer than the Wee Bridge in Dungloe, seven miles from the crime scene.

Back in Meendernasloe, an effort to regain normality had to be made. A terror had struck the community and had manifested itself in stories of the supernatural world which had broken into the normal.[73] People only ventured out in groups after dark, through fear of ghosts.[74] Conell had died violently without a priest.[75] The devil had won his soul in the end. Violent death was regarded as vengeance for living less than an unblemished life. 'Bás gan sagart agus siorraí in ifreann' (Death without a priest and eternity in hell) was the belief.[76] Conell's spirit would now be joined with the devil in hunting more souls. An Annagry man walking on the Annagry to Crolly road one night was crossing 'Píopa Chondaí'[77] when, suddenly, Conell's ghost jumped out of the pipe and told him where the murder weapon and some hidden clothes could be found.[78] Ever after, that section of the road was avoided by all but the brave. Men who were silent were assumed to have hidden knowledge. The long dark nights of the approaching winter did nothing to quell their fears.[79] But the crops in the fields had to be harvested before the October colds set in. Turf had to be brought home and clamped. However, dancing, kaleying and airnéal ceased for, in the darkened skies, in the howling winds, in the harsh heather landscape, the spectre of Conell Boyle enveloped everything.[80]

3. Two scales of justice

Word finally arrived in Meendernasloe during the first week of December 1898 that the trial would open at the winter assizes in Crumlin Road, Belfast within a few days before Lord Chief Justice Sir Peter O'Brien, Bart.[1] This was hardly encouraging news for this was the same 'Peter the Packer' who had manipulated the jury and subjected Fr M'Fadden and the Gweedore people to such unfair procedures in Maryborough. O'Brien was condemned in local folklore during the years following the Maryborough debacle. There was little hope that a fair trial would be forthcoming for Hugh Boyle in Belfast.[2]

On their departure for Belfast the witnesses carried with them the good luck charms traditional to the area, moss from St Dumhach's well in Calhame, some of the 'bratóg Bhríde' cloth from St Brigid's eve night, holy water from Doon Well or other holy wells, and medals dedicated to various saints. The tongs would have been thrown after them on departure from home to wish them good luck.[3]

Despite the intense efforts of the RIC in the area for three months, through visiting houses, checking for dog licences, querying inoculation of children and using any excuse to be among the people in order to gather intelligence or break the code of silence within the area, the small group that assembled to travel to Belfast was testimony to the cohesion of the prevailing silence.[4] No new witnesses and no fresh evidence had been discovered despite the efforts of the RIC.

Lord Chief Justice O'Brien was soon into his stride on Wednesday 7 December 1898 with a varied diary including eight murder cases before him and Hugh's case was listed for the following day. On Thursday afternoon, when Hugh was brought in to the courtroom his neighbours got a shock for he had grown a full beard since they last saw him. He 'was arraigned for, wilfully and with malice aforethought, murdering his father, Conell Boyle, on

15 Lord Chief Justice
Sir Peter O'Brien.

the 30 August last'.[5] A jury was sworn in and the attorney general, in his opening address, set out the Meendernasloe people as a class apart:[6]

> About the middle of June the prisoner got permission from his father to till about two acres of land with oats and potatoes. Disputes seem to have arisen about small and trifling things between them, the character of which the jury would probably assume if they knew how people of this class insisted upon what they considered their rights. If they knew the passion these people had for land and the possession of it they would easily understand the serious enmities that sprang from differences about matters that in their regard seem trifling and unworthy to interrupt the friendship, good-feeling or affection between father and child.[7]

He then outlined his theory that Hugh Boyle came home from Scotland on 30 August via Fintown and walked to Meendernasloe where he killed his father to bring a securer hold on the small patch of land to himself because

> if the father had made a will, the property would have been divided equally among his children.[8] If he got his father out of the way he would have a securer hold on the house and holding besides terminating forever the disputes about the stones and the payment for the cropping.[9]

According to a report in the *Londonderry Sentinel*,

> the accused evinced the greatest interest in all the proceedings of the trial, though otherwise he did not seem to be affected by the serious position in which he is placed. The case has, so far, exhibited exceptional features of interest, at least for the ordinary occupants of a city court. Several of the witnesses displayed a reluctance to converse in English.[10]

The great majority of Meendernasloe people stated in the 1901 census that they spoke both Irish and English and this included most of the trial witnesses but those statements must be put in context, for the reality was that Irish was the common everyday language of the people and they were far from comfortable conducting conversation through English, especially in a Belfast courthouse. The writer, Séamus Ó Grianna from the neighbouring townland of Ranafast in his biography, *Nuair a bhí mé óg*,[11] describes vividly the conflict between the traditional Irish and intruding English, in everyday events during these same years.

This reluctance to speak English soon became a court issue when Margaret Forker was called to give her evidence. She said that, although she knew some English, she knew Irish better and preferred to give her evidence in that language. This brought forth some banter between Sir Peter and the attorney general with his lordship remarking, 'I thought Irish was only spoken, Mr Attorney General, where you and I come from.' The attorney general replied, 'I thought so, my lord,' before turning to Margaret saying, 'We will try English for a while at any rate,' and then proceeded to lead her through her evidence in English.[12] Ellen O'Donnell struggled in English as well, answering, 'I catched his hand,' to one question but when Hugh Boner was called, he was determined to assert his authority on the court and speak in Irish. He was not going to let his people be cowed as the Gweedore people were in Maryborough. He indicated prior to being sworn in that he wanted to give his evidence in Irish, but Mr Atkinson insisted that he give it in English as he had done at the inquest in Meendernasloe. Perhaps remembering Ellen's poor effort, his lordship showed particular empathy with Boner's position saying, 'They do not speak it [English] well and they are afraid. It is the same in the south of Ireland in some parts.'[13]

Despite Boner's protestations, the oath was administered to him in English and Mr Atkinson opened his questioning, 'Were you examined before the court in Irish?' Boner, the father-figure and elder of his people, remained steadfast replying, 'Bhí mé' (I was). Atkinson continued, 'You spoke in English before and you may as well speak in English now. How far do you live from the dead man?' 'Thart faoi dhá chéad slat' (about 200 yards), came the reply. The court admitted defeat. An interpreter was then called and Hugh Boner continued to give the remainder of this evidence through Irish. In local parlance, 'Hugh Boner showed them.' When further witnesses indicated that they wished to speak in Irish there was no problem.

Their victory over the court officials had failed to loosen their tongues though. Co-operation was grudging and reluctant from the Meendernasloe contingent. The dispute between Hugh and Conell over the stones and then over payment for seed was the prosecution's motive for the crime, but they found it an infertile field among the local witnesses. Margaret Forker had never heard of 'any talk between the prisoner and his father about building the new house or about the crops'.[14] Paddy Boner conceded only under intensive questioning that he was at the building of Hugh's house but

> I don't remember what was said at the time. The old man said something that he would not let him take them till he would pay for some debts. I heard him say he would have to pay for the seed potatoes and corn.[15]

Under further questioning Paddy conceded that Hugh 'told me he would have to build a house, that his wife and father did not agree or were not agreeing'. Most of them gave monosyllabic answers but provided little additional information. Mickey Johnny O'Donnell told of sleeping in the same bothey in Scotland as Hugh and sharing their food, but he averred that he never saw him get any letters, nor did he take any notice of his dress on the morning he was leaving nor could he remember if Hugh's trousers were patched. He conceded that Hugh told him 'to tell Mr Whyte that he was going to Edinburgh to see a sick friend and to look for early harvest and that he would be back'.[16] But Hugh had never told him about letters or getting letters. When Mickey was showing some reluctance, his lordship prodded, 'Tell all you can; tell what he said' Mickey replied that Hugh told him he was going to settle some dispute. As to Hugh's return and the information that his father was dead, there seemed remarkably little conversation according to Mickey. Mickey said nothing to Hugh when he gave him the telegram with the information of Conell's death. When Hugh read the telegram, he said nothing. Hugh did not speak at all. Although Hugh was vexed looking, he only said that he was going home. Even when Mickey and Hugh visited Paddy Rogers, who was married to Hugh's sister, Anna, nothing was said in the course of the night except in reply to Roger's question that he had heard of his father's death and, at the end of the night, 'that it was coming up to bed time'.[17] During the following morning, before Hugh departed for his father's funeral, not a word had passed between the two men. Mickey, however, did concede that Hugh had a parcel tied with a red handkerchief when he returned after being absent for four days.[18]

The Meendernasloe group could be happy with their day's work. None of them had been broken by the court and they conceded very little evidence. They had kept their answering as short as possible and professed ignorance on most questions. That they had been acting as a group, determined to impose their own standards of right and dignity, and resolved to conceal their inner thoughts and knowledge, was obvious. Paddy Boner might have said too much about the stones and the seed, and Mickey Johnny would have been better not to mention the parcel or the dispute, but not one piece of evidence placed Hugh in the townland during the time of his father's death. The secrets of their internal world remained as obscure to the court and the jury when they finished their evidence as when they began. Whatever the court might discover in other ways, nothing would be forthcoming from them. Their reluctance was put in stark contrast by the effusive testimony given by the 11 witnesses from the Fintown area who placed Hugh in various parts of the district from his arrival on the Tuesday preceding Conell's death and his departure on Wednesday's train to Derry. The methodical diligence of the RIC police-work in linking each piece of evidence with testimony and witnesses only served to compare the lack of co-operation they had received from the people in Meendernasloe. Their answers were full and frank. Their recollections were clear. They had no doubts but that the man's identity was Hugh Boyle. What he ate, what he drank, what he said, what he wore, and how he looked were all remembered in detail. The carmen brought him as far as the Wee Bridge near Dungloe, seven miles from Meendernasloe, but not one step closer than that.[19]

Three months of RIC work had produced nothing. Seven members of the RIC then gave evidence. Principal among them was District Inspector Bell and deep controversy arose as to the manner in which the statement was taken from Hugh on the night of his arrival. O'Brien listened to all the argument and decided to defer a decision on its admissibility.

Sophie Deegan was then called. Her presence gave the Meendernasloe people some anxiety, for she had allied herself with the RIC at the beginning by confirming that she could identify the various handwriting in the letters between Mary Harley, Conell and Hugh. Her ability to confirm the passage of letters and identify handwriting would be vital evidence in the case. However, they need not have feared. Sophie had undergone a change of attitude and she repeatedly told the court, 'I could not swear it' in answer to their many queries. Months earlier, she had signed a statement that she knew Hugh's handwriting but now she 'could not swear it'. Despite much prompting, Sophie continued to reply to each question, 'I could not swear it.' Exasperated, the prosecution then asked her if she had been 'talking to any of the Boyle people' and she admitted that she had been talking to Charley Boyle.[20] On the conclusion of her evidence another milestone had been passed. Sophie had re-established her membership of the local community by retracting her original evidence and refusing to make any disclosure of help to the court. As the Irish saying goes, 'Níor thug sí cúl le cine' (She did not renege on her kin).

Hugh's brother, Charley, told how he had written to Hugh in June telling him to come over to Inch's Farm in Scotland. He himself had gone to Scotland in June 1897. Hugh used to send money to his father, of whom he never heard him speak an ill word. He knew of no dispute. Hugh never told him of any disagreement nor did he say he was going to Ireland to settle a dispute. He had never seen Hugh get letters from his wife nor did he read him a letter from his father. They never spoke of his father or the people at home; nothing was ever said about relations between Conell and Mary Harley; they never spoke of crops at home; he could give no evidence about the clothes Hugh was wearing. In fact Charley was the least forthcoming of all the witnesses. He gave the court no information.[21]

Whatever differences the Harleys had with their neighbours at home were shelved for the court appearance. These would be dealt with back in Meendernasloe. Mary Harley's mother, Margaret, held the line of ignorance and silence. She was little better than Charley in her testimony. She was careful to assert that Mary and herself slept in the same bed on the Tuesday night of the murder so that she could give Mary an alibi. She was not aware of any differences or disputes and she had never spoken to Conell about the crops. Only when it was put to her that her daughter had dug the potatoes did Margaret become animated. 'She was belied. People said she did but she did not.' She did not know of any falling out between Mary and Conell. She did not know if Mary had brought Hugh's letters over to Conell. Margaret did not see or know much or, if she did, she did not tell the court.[22]

The RIC had built one of the most comprehensive cases possible. They had presented more than 35 witnesses who produced a line of evidence bringing the prisoner from the farm in Eddleston, Scotland to the Wee Bridge in Dungloe, with every piece of evidence linked comprehensively in the chain. But at the Wee Bridge their chain ended. After 5 p.m. on that late August evening, from the Wee Bridge to Meendernasloe, nobody could be found who would swear that he or she had seen Hugh Boyle within the area. Neither could they produce a witness who would testify that there had been serious disagreement between Hugh, his wife Mary and his father. Nobody saw anything or heard anything which might assist the RIC. Meendernasloe, from within, was not an individualistic society. Kinship, language, instinctive feelings of belonging, inter-dependence and illiteracy bound the community in a local identity and generated a 'mentality' within, which was denied to those outside. That 'mentalité' dictated that the outside world would gain no admission to the shorthand of their internal world. Whatever their differences or divisions, they had gone to Belfast and had stood firm against the forces of the government and the official world. The RIC and the law had failed to breech their impenetrable world. Whatever the rights or wrongs of Hugh Boyle's actions his own community would deal with it in their own way.

On Saturday, the lord chief justice entered the courtroom to sum up. Hugh, who exhibited little interest in the latter stages of his trial, looked careworn and pale as he entered the court but he seemed to realise more keenly that day the gravity of his position.[23] Mr Gallagher addressed the jury on Hugh's behalf. The case for the crown rested altogether and entirely on circumstantial evidence. There was no testimony to confirm that the prisoner was the man left at Dungloe Wee Bridge on 30 August. Neither was there any positive identification at Fintown. The young ladies might be unintentionally mistaken. If he were a murderer, would he give way to emotion when he heard the news of his father's death, in Scotland? There was no evidence of malice. There was no motive proved on the part of the crown. Conell Boyle came to his death by manslaughter, and not by murder. The party had stunned the deceased, and then, in his fright, dragged him into the household and ran away. Whether Conell Boyle was manslaughtered or not, there was no evidence to connect the prisoner by act or by word in his death. As the crown had failed to prove the case, the prisoner was entitled to the verdict of the jury.[24]

Mr Henry replied for the crown. If they considered the offence could be regarded as one of a minor degree, the prosecution sought no victim from them. Whether the verdict was manslaughter or not, the crown would be satisfied. This willingness of the prosecution to accept the lesser charge of manslaughter together with its concession to exclude Hugh's statement (taken by D.I. Bell) must have been heartening to Hugh and to his supporters in the court. At worst a manslaughter charge would have a fixed jail term of perhaps five years and perhaps, with pleas for leniency, might have been even less.

The main point in O'Brien's summing up was the probability of the prisoner's visit home being only for the purpose of remonstrance with his father, and that something then arose between them in consequence of which he killed unintentionally was strongly argued in the prisoner's favour.[25]

He strongly pointed to manslaughter throughout so that the court had no doubt as to O'Brien's desired verdict. The Meendernasloe listeners must have been astonished at the divergence between the generosity of the Peter O'Brien who sat before them and the infamy of 'Peter the Packer' in Donegal folklore. The jury retired at 12.30 p.m. Ten minutes later, they returned to court and the foreman asked had any witness proof that the window was whole on Tuesday evening.[26] Hugh Boner (again insisting that he would only answer in Irish), Margaret Forker and Ellen O'Donnell were recalled in turn and each told the court that they had not noticed the window broken before the murder but they were rather uncertain. The jury retired once again but it appears that his lordship was becoming worried by their attitude for, despite his many references to manslaughter during his previous address, they seemed more deeply immersed in the analysis than he would have liked. Almost immediately, he recalled them to the court and told them that if they thought there was a dispute between Conell and Hugh, and that the prisoner struck the deceased, without going there with the intention of killing him, that would be manslaughter. Four more times, O'Brien mentioned the word manslaughter and on each occasion pointed out the various actions by the prisoner which would result in that verdict. He left few options uncovered. Once more, it was obvious that he was exercising extreme leniency towards the prisoner on this occasion. He wanted a manslaughter verdict. The jury again retired, and returned to court at 2.30 p.m. Almost mechanically, Hugh stood up, resting his left hand on the front of the dock.[27] The foreman announced a verdict of 'guilty of murder' but strongly recommended the prisoner to mercy on account of his youth. Hugh made no reply for he seemed dazed.[28]

His lordship said, It becomes my duty now – the most painful duty that can be imposed upon man – to pass the most dreadful sentence of the law upon you. The sentence of the court is, and I do hereby adjudge and order that you, Hugh Boyle, be taken from the bar of this court, where you now stand, to the place from whence you came, her majesty's prison, in and for the county of Antrim and from thence to her majesty's prison in the county of Londonderry and that you be kept there until Thursday, the twelfth day of January which shall be the year of Our Lord, 1899 (his Lordship here assumed the black cap) and that you be taken on that day to the common place of execution within the

walls of the said prison in which you shall be then confined, and that
you be then and there, hanged by the neck until you are dead and that
your body be buried within the precincts of the prison in which you
shall be then confined; and may the Lord have mercy on your soul.[29]

At this Hugh reeled backward and fell into the arms of the warders, who
removed him from the court.[30]

It is said locally that the witnesses and neighbours from Meendernasloe who
were in the court when this verdict was announced were stunned and awe-struck.
Their calculations had gone astray for, unlike the case in Maryborough, they had
been wrong-footed, not by a biased judge or devious court officials, but by 12
ordinary men from the city of Belfast who read their conspiracy of silence in an
unexpected manner. Reading in the papers about murder and execution had
prepared none of them for the fact that one of their own, who had grown up in
conditions more harsh than many, was now to be hanged. A period in prison
would be acceptable, but the raw finality of Hugh Boyle dangling at the end of
a rope was incomprehensible. Even those from the Fintown area who had given
evidence of identification and movement were full of regret at the announcement
of the verdict, and it is said that many of them regretted their evidence.[31]

Hugh was put on the five o'clock train from Belfast and arrived in Derry at
8.25 p.m. on Saturday night. 'The condemned man was greatly affected on his
way to Derry and wept bitterly almost the whole journey.'[32] The Meendernasloe
people took the train to Strabane and then to Fintown. It is said that some of
them had not stopped weeping when they arrived shocked, distressed and
exhausted in Meendernasloe.[33] In Derry gaol, prisoner number 826, Hugh
Boyle[34]

> occupied the condemned cell, being visible to no one except the
> chaplain, doctor and warders. He exercised unseen by his fellow prisoners
> and even attended mass without their being aware of his presence in the
> prison chapel. This is rendered possible owing to the construction of the
> building.[35]

On 17 December 1898, a letter from James Boyle, coroner for West
Donegal, was sent to the lord lieutenant of Ireland, Dublin Castle.

> It is my firm opinion and conviction that the condemned man never
> *intended* to murder his father. No doubt, he came across on an impulse,
> to settle some paltry dispute between his wife and his father; that heat
> was engendered at their meeting and a scuffle ensued; and, that as a
> result, the unfortunate man Connell Boyle met his death …
>
> I may state that the two doctors who performed the post mortem
> examination agreed with me that murder was never intended and, I

16 Prisoner Hugh Boyle, November 1901.

have no doubt, that if Mr Bell DI who so successfully traced up the limits of the case went to express an opinion, he would not dissent.[36]

On 19 December 1898, Lord Chief Justice O'Brien, wrote to the lord lieutenant's office:

> In my opinion the death sentence in this case of Hugh Boyle should be commuted to one of Penal Servitude for life. I am clearly of opinion that he killed his father but I think the instrument, with which the blows which caused death were inflicted from, owed more to a sudden quarrel than to the deliberate purpose of death. The instrument was a comparatively light one and seems to have been picked up in the street – not such a one as prisoner would probably have used if intent in deliberate murder.[37]

It was now time for the 'quality' in north-west Donegal, those who formed public opinion and 'common sense', to enter their plea for mercy. Nine priests of the three parishes of the Rosses and Gweedore allied to 22 members of the shopocracy of the same parishes signed a petition pleading for mercy and forwarded it to Lord Cadogan, the lord lieutenant.[38] On 22 December 1898, Cadogan decided that, 'in view of the letter of the Lord Chief Justice and having conferred with the Lord Chancellor, that the said Hugh Boyle be kept in Penal Servitude for the term of his natural life'. Following an order made on 28 December, Hugh was transferred permanently to Maryborough prison, in Queens county where he joined Michael Cleary,[39] the 'mad Lynchehaun'[40] and the Maamtrasna prisoners.[41]

The machinery of the centralized state had dealt with an offender according to its code of justice, but in Meendernasloe there was a second scale by which the events of the night of 30 August had to be measured. The jury was the local community, those who refused to divulge the shorthand of their mentality to the outside world in 1898. The code under which each was tried was the tradition, conventions and accepted ways of generations. No court sitting took place and there was no judge but the will of the people and their community conscience. Their conclusion conceded that Conell Boyle was a difficult, hard and tight-fisted man who had fallen out with his son, Charley and could not even tolerate his own daughter, Anna, in his house. Hugh was the only one left and he pushed him to get married in order to have a woman look after himself and the house and land in his old age. But it was an unfortunate choice. Mary Harley and he had no chance of reconciliation, for she was a self-centred, strong-willed, persuasive young woman not given to compromise or direction. There were fights about the building of the house and the stones and the crops and, when Hugh went to Scotland, things became worse. It is accepted by the community that Mary Harley drove Hugh to the point of distraction with her letters constantly detailing Conell's threats towards her. Hugh came home on the evening of the Gweedore Fair and went to his father's house in the company of Mary Harley and her sister. In a society dependant on the resolution of conflict by physical means rather than more refined methods, it was only natural that Hugh challenged Conell at the door, but the father was a man of quick temper and with a few drinks in him after the fair, he was not in the mood for compromise. He attacked his son, who also had some drink taken, and, being a stronger man, wrestled him to the ground and pinned him there. At this point, Mary Harley's sister put her apron around Conell's head and called to Mary to get a stick. While Conell held Hugh beneath him, Mary pummelled his head with the stave of the barrel until he was dead. They then dragged him inside and, at Mary's insistence, Hugh took off for Scotland.[42]

There are inconsistencies in this analysis. First, Hugh Boyle stated in Fintown that he had not eaten since the previous day, which would have excluded him from visiting his wife's home on the night of the murder. Secondly, the medical evidence stated that the barrel-stave had blood and hair on it which would rule out wounds inflicted through an apron. Thirdly, if Mary Harley had been present at the scene, she would almost certainly have taken the bloodstained trousers and disposed of them rather than have Hugh bring them back to Scotland in a parcel. Fourthly, this account is highly favourable to Hugh Boyle in that he is portrayed as a young, immature man in the grip of malicious women. However, in the local mentality with its dominant masculinity, the Harley women were the more guilty party, and the story is still told that, when Hugh Boyle was dying, his last words were that he did not murder his father. It is also said locally that many, many years later, when Mary Harley's sister lay on her death-bed in a coma, a neighbour who was looking after her, continued to whisper in her ear at every opportunity, 'Cé 'mharaigh Conall Húdaí Bhaoill?' (Who killed Conell Boyle?) The dying woman, however, made no response and the great secret of the events of that night died with her.[43] Mary Harley played Eve in this Eden's garden, according to the surviving local oral accounts. The community believed that she had failed in her duty as a wife. She refused to make a home for a widowed man who took her into his house as any good woman should have done. She had caused trouble and dissension within a family by her cunning and deviousness. Hugh would never have murdered his father but for the urging of Mary Harley. That she might have loved him passionately was neither in their understanding nor in their vocabulary. Her refusal to bow to the code of the community excluded her from participation within it. Her presence at home would forever be a reminder of the crime and an obstacle in the marriage chances of her siblings and an affront to her family and kin.

Within a year Mary was in Bayonne, New Jersey,[44] where she was to stay without return for almost 30 years. In 1902 she wrote the following letter to the king on behalf of her husband:[45]

> To His Royal Highness,
>
> Your Honour,
>   I am going to write you a few lines to let you understand my great, great, trouble, in which I am in and I beg of you honour that you will grant me one favour which I am asking of you for your sake and for God sake. It is the only favour I ever ask and I trust in the Lord that your Honour will try and do something now. I am begging for God's sake of you to try and release my husband and let him come to me to this country and I will pray for you night and day. It would content me if I would only know that my husband would be released in one year from now. I am going to leave my sorrow and trouble in your hand. Trusting the Lord that you would take pity of a sore broken hearted woman like me, a sorry bird alone in this country not able to make a living for myself. The only favour I ask is to get my dear husband once more.
>   I earnestly beg of your Royal Highness to write for me as I know you are the only one of earth that can do anything for me. And trusting in God that you will have luck and prosperity in every thing you undertake.
>   Your Royal Highness, I am going to explain my trouble and sorrow to you which I hope that you will take pity on me. I am a young woman and was married when I was only 17 years of age in 1898 and

my husband was only 22 (years) of age. And in 1899 he was committed
for the murder of his father which I am sure he never had anything to
do with it. And he was taken away to Mountjoy Prison and he is now
transferred to Queen's County Prison.

And Your Honour, I had to leave my home and come out to this
country 2 years ago and I have lost my health in this country and I
don't like to go back home again. So I am here among strangers
without a friend in the world, only my husband [at] home I loved so
dearly and home I cannot see me.

Just one little note and tell me what you can do for my dear
husband. I will think the time long until I get a note.

I therefore must close my note as I hope your honour will excuse
my bad writing for I am doing the best I can.

From Mary Boyle

To His Royal Highness

King Edward vii.

This is my own address:
Mrs. Mary Boyle,
C/o Mr. John Sharkey,
No. 31E, 18th St,
Bayonne,
New Jersey,
U.S. America.

An examination of Mary Boyle's birth certificate would show that she was
born on 26 November 1877 and was 20 years and three months when she got
married.

In 1906 Mary wrote to Hugh:[46]

My Dearest Dear,

With pleasure I am writing you a few lines in answer to your (letter)
which I received some time ago all right. Glad you are feeling well as
I am only poorly myself. Well dear you will be sorry to hear that after
all my hard earning since I came to this country, that I wasn't two
weeks out of a place since, well dear, what do you think but the bank
that I had all my money in that I had, I am sorry to say that it is
bankrupt and busted about three weeks ago and hasn't the slightest
hopes of ever getting one cent out of it. Well dear, I am so miserable
over the head of it that I really don't care what will become of me now

when I was working hard and trying to save something to have in my old day. To see me now just as far away as I was when I came here but really I don't see anything for me in this world but trouble.

Well, my dearest little sweetheart, when you were taken away from me before I was nineteen years of age, you the only one I ever care for or loved on this earth. I thought then that no one would ever live through what I came through but myself. Also I felt so that nothing would ever bother my brain again but now you can imagine how I feel now dear. I don't want you to worry about me as I know you got your trials in this world but I cannot help but tell you my trouble as I haven't no one else to tell them to. But I guess I will have to bear it all. There's many a poor family that has lost their's as well so when I have the health I guess I don't need to complain although I don't feel very good since the day you were taken away from me. I never was the same since. And the day I heard of the bank bursted was a trial on me.

My dearest husband, your letter was very sweet and caused me to shed many tears while reading it. I am glad you are feeling well dear. Don't trouble yourself writing to anybody for they are not worth writing to. In your next letter tell me do you think you will ever get out. I don't see why dear, that they don't let you come to me and make me feel happy from all sorrows as there is no other one on earth but you that could make me happy. If I only got a message to go to meet you, dear little sweetheart I think I would be the gladdest one on the earth today. But I guess I will have to wait a long while. However let us hope for the best. Think of the future and forget the past. I wonder if you miss me dear as much as I miss you. I wonder if you cherish the love that we once knew. I wonder if your love is just as true. I wonder if you miss me as much as I miss you.

I must tell you that I had a letter from home. My brother is in Scotland. Rosey has another baby boy. You know they are living at home now. My sister Bridget got four boys. They are getting along good. Did I ever tell you old Peggy Boyle died last Winter. Andy Rogers is for death. I haven't seen Sharkey since he got buckled up but in fact I would not speak to him or never would also.

I hope you will write to me just as soon as you get permission to do so as I will be waiting to hear from you.

I will close my long letter with love and best wishes from your dear little wife Mary to my husband, Hugh Boyle

With deepest love dear I close this letter

From yours to death.

Address the same but hope you don't think it strange to address my letter in my own name dear.

No. 106 Heberton Ave,

Port Richmond,
St. Island
New York,
U.S.A.

Excuse writing and all the mistakes.
Write me a long letter.
Goodbye dear.

If presented to the communal jury of Meendernasloe these two letters would only serve to prove to her detractors that she was a devious, self-centred woman and to her supporters as a woman of intense, genuine love and passion. However, the traditional full generation was to pass before she ventured back home for a short visit. Even then she was reminded of her past. On her return she is reputed to have worn the first nail varnish seen in the Annagry locality. The old people stared in astonishment at the 'blood' covering her nails and averred that no matter how she washed her hands, the blood was there again each morning.[47] Though never exonerated by the local community, Mary made sporadic holiday visits until her death in America in the 1960s.

Anna Rogers, Conell's sister, who lived some miles from Meendernasloe, took to religion in a big way. Her husband Paddy – he who spent some time studying for the priesthood – came out to meet the Annagry postman one day to ask if he had seen Anna. The postman replied that he had seen her at Annagry chapel. Paddy shook his head and said: 'It's a pity I didn't become a priest for the first thing I would have done is abolish the nine Fridays.'

Charley Boyle acquired Conell's farm but departed immediately for America. In 1903, the two houses and the land were legally transferred to Johnny Boyle, Conell's brother,[48] and remained in the family thereafter, though neither house was ever occupied. Charley never came back home. His crime was that of association. He would have been excluded from the meitheal, ignored by the community and would be unacceptable as a marriage partner. In the old Irish proverb, 'Is fada siar a théann iarsma an drochbhirt' (An evil deed has a deep antiquity).[49]

Year after year, Hugh Boyle wrote his petition for mercy, pleading his regret and remorse for the deed he had done. His last petition of 1909 probably told most of the truth about his father's murder:

> I was in Scotland close upon three months when I received a letter from my wife who told me that my father had threatened her if she would lay a hand on the crops I put in that he would cut the head off her and the following day I received a proof of this from himself. And

as I knew my father's temper I came home. But I could stand before my Almighty Judge and say that I never intended to hurt a hair upon his head. When I arrived at home I met my father at the house as he was putting in a cow and his first word to me was what the damnation brought you here. I told him he was the real cause of bringing me here: He then put the cow in to the byre and I went into the house. Soon after he came in and ordered me to leave the house, rising the stick above me, I made a grasp at the stick and both of us fell against the window. I been stronger I twisted it out of his hands upon which he ran to a heap of stones that was lying opposite the door. I saw if he got one my life would be in danger. I struck him a random blow and he fell upon the stones. I can assure Your Excellency that it was all done upon the impulse of the moment. I took him up and brought him in. I then ran to my new house. I found no one there. I confess to God I did not know what I was doing. I went back to Scotland again – and been so that I did not care what would happen me at that time. I came home again and was arrested.[50]

He was released from Maryborough prison on 7 September 1909 and went immediately to Bayonne, where Mary was still waiting for him. They opened a boarding house there. He is remembered as being very quiet and often used to say to his guests, many of whom were from Annagry, 'Be good to your father and mother.'[51] He fulfilled the words he had uttered in Gweedore barracks many years earlier about banishment. He never met his brother Charley again, and he never returned to Ireland. He died in the 1940s.[52]

The final cleansing of the parish was undertaken by the church. The Redemptorist order held a six-week mission, the second within two years, which is remembered as 'An Misiún Mór' (Great Mission) for its reverberations continued for years afterwards through the fear it instilled in the people. The mission was in Annagry (its first ever mission) from 8 to 22 December 1901 where 'the Catholic population amounts to 3,000'. The people of Annagry were found to be 'insatiable in their desire to hear sermons and to approach the Sacraments. Irish is universally spoken here. The state of the people is good although there is some intemperance ... owing to the introduction of Scotch customs, especially drinking on a Saturday night.' About 2,300 confessions were heard and about 3000 communions were served.[53] The Sacred Heart Sodality was established and about 800 members were enrolled. About 500 joined St Patrick's Total Abstinence League.[54]

But according to local belief, vengeance was to be the Lord's due also. It is said locally that Mary and Hugh had one child only but that child was so deformed and unnatural that it was taken from them immediately after birth and put in a home and was never seen again.[55] People who knew them in Bayonne aver that they were childless,[56] which would probably be interpreted as the curse operating, only in a different manner, by someone knotting the

string during their wedding ceremony. But the belief of the local people was
not to be diminished either. The seers and sages of the traditional inheritance
in Meendernasloe would ascertain that Hugh Boyle only fulfilled his destiny
for he was cursed in his own right. He was born during a full eclipse of the
moon and the midwife attending the birth did everything possible to delay
the baby's arrival until the eclipse had passed. Her efforts were unsuccessful,
however and, when the new-born infant arrived, the midwife is said to have
held him in her arms and ruefully remarked, 'Rachaidh do gháir níos faide ná
do chois.' (Your infamy will go further than your foot).[57] In the local
tradition, it was inevitable that misfortune would befall Hugh Boyle, and the
murder of his father was the fulfilment of this curse.

Conclusion

The great montage of nineteenth-century Ireland with juxtaposed representations of the great events, each with illuminated heroes or shadowed traitors, is brushed onto the canvas of the Irish landscape in blending hues and contrasting shades, all in a powerful maelstrom of movement, energy and change. Our eyes are drawn to the focal centre by the strong tones of union, religion, secret societies, agrarianism, emancipation, reform, repeal, famine, fenianism, disestablishment and home rule and the characters that have shaped destinies- O'Connell, Davis, Davitt, Parnell, Croke, Cullen and Gladstone among others, all beneath the dominating edifice of Dublin Castle, and surrounded by masses of people in the central vanguard of the assembly. When our eyes tire of the impressive scene we avert our gaze to the periphery of the canvas where the fading colours merge into a background of misted anonymity and distant obscurity, and it is here that a bland and uninteresting Meendernasloe might be faintly discernible to an inquisitive eye. It might have remained forever at the ashen margins of the canvas of Irish life with its people peripheral to the mainstream of the ever-centralizing world of church and state, devoid of position, famous names, rich resources or coveted possessions, jealously guarding its inherited treasures of language, culture, customs and lifestyle and resisting the tides of change pounding on its shores but for the death of Conell Boyle on the night of 30 August 1898. That death brought together the two great tidal movements of Irish life in the latter nineteenth century. One was the extension of central government – Catholic church and developing economy increasingly filling the hidden nooks and remote inlets of peripheral Ireland with energising motion, strength and virulence. Each ebbing tide carried away forever into the great ocean some of the vital lifeblood and cherished ways of the old community.

Conell Boyle's death set these two aspects of Irish life in conflict. The apparatus of state, operating in clear clinical systems, identified one defendant who was brought through its processes and was eventually found guilty and condemned, first to death and later to penal servitude for life and had done so through the RIC, magistrates, attorneys and solicitors, magisterial investigations and assize courts with court records, written statements, expert witnesses, cross-examinations, and challenged evidence to substantiate the case against this one man amid a welter of newspaper publicity. When Hugh Boyle walked out of Maryborough gaol the state's involvement in the crime and its punishment was closed for good. The Meendernasloe people had been reluctantly and unwillingly dragged into this encroaching world for a brief period, but they withheld their co-operation from it before re-entering into the receding culture at home where the process for the determination of guilt was to be measured according to their own ways. In a creeping silence the application of their justice would be very different but equally ruthless. There were no investigations, no statements, no court sittings, no records and no newspaper publicity. Precedence and custom formed through the past generations had set the guidelines to determine the fall-out of justice. In a society where individualism was intolerable, it was inconceivable that only one person would take responsibility for an offence within the community. A person was recognized as part of a kin-group and the tentacles of their justice would expand to envelop all those who were associated with the crime. Within a year, Mary Harley was in exile and Charley soon emigrated for good. Hugh Boyle followed them on release and was never to return. Two homes were closed and were dismantled, stone by stone, until they were invisible through the gorse and growth. Whin bushes were let cover the hillside to erase the memories of unhappy homes and corrupted soil. The sentence of the local community would percolate through the minds and memories of the local people for generations to come.

Since the days of the great tragedy, nature has been drawing the soil of the tiny fields back to the original bogland state from which it was fashioned. The two little houses on the deserted and forlorn slope of Meendernasloe hill have been knocked to their foundations and their stones formed into boundary walls. On a summer's day, neighbours' eyes are more likely to be drawn to the hillside, not by the lichened, grey stones but by the inviting cloak of fragrant, yellow-tipped furze. New bungalows continue to cover the townland with entrance gates and doorbells advertising the new privacy and independence. Rooftop aerials and satellite dishes bring in the global cultures that raise the horizons and detach the populace from the purely local tribalism of former days. Almost anything can be spoken of nowadays. Well, almost anything but not quite everything. One topic is still too sensitive, too raw, too recent and too invasive to be mentioned aloud. Nobody notices the two little remnant ruins on the hillside but yet they dominate the landscape and keep sentinel watch over the ghostly memories and recollections of the people. Only in hushed and whispering tones will anyone yet mention the murder of Conell Boyle.

Notes

Conell Boyle, widower, had two sons, Hugh and Charles, and one daughter, Anna.

Hugh married his neighbour, Mary Harley.

Anna married Patrick Rodgers.

Charles was unmarried and lived in Scotland for most of the time.

Conell Boyle's sister, Mary, was married to Hugh Bonner and they lived about 200 yards from Conell's house.

Their daughter, Margaret, who was married to Daniel Forker, and their son, Patrick, were living with them at the time of the murder.

Another daughter, Nancy, was married to James O'Donnell and they lived about one mile away.

James and Nancy's daughter, Ellen O'Donnell, lived with the Bonner grandparents for much of the time.

ABBREVIATIONS

CDB	Congested Districts Board
CRF	Convict Reference Files in National Archives, Dublin.
DJ	*Derry Journal*
DS	*Derry Standard*
LS	*Londonderry Sentinel*
NA	National Archives
NLI	National Library of Ireland
Transcripts	Transcripts of the shorthand notes taken during the trial of Hugh Boyle at the Winter Assizes in Belfast. Located in NA, CRF

INTRODUCTION

1 The Rosses was the name given to the combined civil parishes of Templecrone and Lettermacaward, in north west Donegal.

2 For a good insight into this community towards the end of the nineteenth century see Séamus Ó Grianna, *Nuair a bhí mé óg* (Cork, 1979 reprint) and Fionn Mac Cumhaill, *Na Rosa go brách* (Dublin, 1939). See also the novels of Séamus Ó Grianna, *Caisleáin óir* (Cork, 1976, reprint) and *Cith is dealán* (Cork, 1976, reprint).

3 James Hack Tuke, *Irish distress and its remedies* (London, 1880), p. 22.

4 Census of Ireland, 1891; CDB Rosses Baseline report, 1892.

5 The parish of Templecrone was divided in two in 1836. Lower Templecrone became the parish of the northern half of the Rosses. It is often called Kincasslagh parish because the

parish church is situated in Kincasslagh.

6 NLI, *Evicted Tenants Commission,* 1893, vol. ii, p. 354.
7 To west Donegal people the Lagan meant the good farmland between the Donegal mountains and the Sperrin mountains.
8 CDB, Baseline report 'The Rosses,' 1892, p. 8.
9 Ben O'Donnell, *The story of the Rosses* (Lifford, 1999), pp 184–85.
10 Ó Grianna, *Nuair a bhí mé óg,* p. 27.
11 Ibid., pp 29–31.
12 Ibid., pp 96–7.
13 Séamus Ó Grianna, *Saol corrach* (Cork, reprint 1981), pp 7–26.
14 Ó Grianna, *Saol corrach,* p. 20.
15 CDB Baseline report, 'The Rosses', 1892, p. 10.
16 Jim Mac Loughlin, 'The politics of nation-building in post-Famine Donegal' in William Nolan, Liam Ronayne and Mairéad Dunlevy (eds.), *Donegal history and society* (Dublin, 1995), pp 585–86. (Hereafter *Donegal history.*)
17 The Public Health (Ireland) Act 1878 gave rise to many new health initiatives.
18 *LS,* 24 Sept. 1898, p. 4.
19 CDB Baseline report, 'The Rosses', p. 1.
20 Seán Ó Súilleabháin, *Irish folk custom and belief* (Cork, 1967), p. 13.
21 Angela Bourke, *The burning of Bridget Cleary* (London, 1999), p. 209.
22 Jarlath Waldron, *Maamtrasna* (Dublin, 1992), p. 11.
23 NA, Convict Reference Files (CRF), misc.1524–1910, (Hugh Boyle), 3/786/5311. (Hereafter CRF.)
24 Redemptorist Order, Esker, Athenry, Co. Galway, Domestic Archives, Mission chronicle, vol. 1, 1899–1909, (Hereafter Esker Archives.)
25 Irish Folklore Commission, University College, Dublin. (Hereafter IFC.)
26 Voluntary group of workers, usually men.

1. THE WORLD OF CONELL BOYLE

1 *DJ,* 5 Sept. 1898, 'The tragedy in county Donegal,' Hugh Boner's evidence.
2 NA, Griffith's Valuation, Parish of Templecrone (Dublin, 1851), pp 153–4.
3 NA, Census of population 1901, Co. Donegal, Annagary DED, no. 55; townland of Meendernasloe, no. 13.
4 NA, Griffith's Valuation 1851 and Census of population 1841 and 1901, townland of Annagary, no.1.
5 NA, Griffith's Valuation 1851. The shop was owned by Patrick McGinley of Mullaghdoo.
6 NA, Census 1901, Annagary DED no. 55, townland of Annagary, No. 1.
7 Fionn Mac Cumhaill, *Na Rosa go brách* (Dublin, 1939), pp 10–18. References to Caimí, the shopkeeper, throughout the book illustrates the power and influence of such people in the Rosses community. See also CDB, the Rosses, p. 8.
8 NA, Census 1901, Co. Donegal, Annagary DED, no. 55, townland of Meendernasloe, 15.
9 NA, Census 1901.
10 *DJ,* 9 Dec. 1898, 'The Donegal Murder,' prosecution statement at trial.
11 *Donegal history,* pp 641–2.
12 Rabble was the name given to the Letterkenny fair, held on the Friday after 12 May and 12 November each year.
13 CDB Rosses, p. 5.
14 CDB, Rosses, p. 8. The Scottish and Lagan earnings accounted for 37 per cent of the household budget in the Rosses in 1892.
15 Local Oral Sources, source B and trial transcripts, p. 162, evidence of Charley Boyle.
16 *DJ,* 5 Oct. 1898, p. 7.
17 Valuation Office, cancellation books, townland of Meendernasloe. Griffith's Valuation lists Hugh Boyle as one of 40 partners holding 722 acres between them in 1835.
18 CDB Rosses, p. 11.
19 Ibid.
20 Author's survey of marriages in Annagry D.E.E.
21 I.F.C. Ms 322. Pádraig Ó Rabhartaigh, p. 510.
22 Local Oral Sources, source E.
23 Local Oral Sources, source B.
24 CDB Rosses, p. 11. See also Seán O'Suilleabhain, *Irish wake amusements* (Cork, 1967).
25 CDB Rosses, p. 11.

26 Local Oral Sources, source E.

27 IFC, John Boyle, his grandson recorded some of these stories for the IFC in Loughanure N.S., 1939. IFC, national school series, County Donegal, Loughanure N.S., 1939.

28 Ó Grianna, *Nuair a bhí mé óg*, 'Oíche thaibhseoireachta,' pp 114–23.

29 Séamus Ó Grianna, *Caisleáin óir* (Cork, 1976), pp 55–8.

30 Local Oral Sources, source F.

31 The Letterkenny and Burtonport Extension Railway (L&BER) opened March 1903.

32 *LS*, 24 May 1898, p. 7.

33 *DS*, 27 Jan. 1898, 'Meeting at Burtonport.'

34 CDB Rosses, p. 3.

35 *DJ*, 5 Sept. 1898, 'The Donegal Murder,' evidence of Hugh O'Donnell.

36 Agricultural statistics, 1898, H.C. 1899 cvi, p. 62.

37 *DS*, Nov. 1899 in an editorial stated, 'Dungloe Summer Fair, held on the 4th June, was always known as "The Fighting Fair," for over a century, lived up to its name.'

38 *DJ*, 21 Feb. 1898, p. 8.

39 NA, CBS-DCCI files – 3/716, northern division, carton 6, Jan to May 1895, Feb report.

40 *DJ*, 21 Feb. 1898, p. 8.

41 *DS*, editorial, November 1899.

42 C.D.B., Rosses, p. 10.

43 *Evicted Tenants Commission*, 1893, vol. ii, pp 374–82.

44 Ibid., p. 383. Revd James McFadden served one term and Revd Stephens two terms in prison.

45 Ibid., Revd James McFadden's evidence, pp 375–82.

46 Pádraig Ua Cnáimhsí, *Idir an dá ghaoth* (Dublin, 1997), p. 230.

47 Name given to drivers of horses and sidecars.

48 Ua Cnáimhsí, *Idir an dá ghaoth*, p. 231.

49 Ibid.

50 Ibid.

51 Paul McGeady, *A short history of Gaoth Dobhair*, (Donegal, undated), p. 21.

52 McGeady, *A short history*, p. 21.

53 Ibid.

54 Seán Ac Fhionnlaoich, *Scéal Ghaoth Dobhair* (Dublin, 1983), pp 121–22.

55 CDB Rosses, p. 10.

56 Ó Grianna, *Nuair a bhí mé óg*, 'an misean', pp 85–93. The parish priest was unhappy that the people did not understand a mission held in Annagry at the turn of the century because it was conducted in English. Irish-speaking priests were booked for a second mission two years later. But they spoke with deep Munster Irish for the week. Hardly a word was understood. Some people thought they were speaking in English and most thought they were speaking in Latin.

57 Ó Grianna, *Nuair a bhí mé óg*, pp 26–34, 'an tseanscoil' and pp 35–44, 'lá an easbaig.' This autobiographical work gives a vivid picture of the suffering endured while learning of catechism through English in Ranafast N.S. close to Meendernasloe, in the parish of Lower Templecrone at the turn of the century and the fear of failure before the bishop on confirmation day. The author sets out the local language and belief in contrast to that of the church.

58 I.F.C., Ms. 322, expands on these practices in Meendernasloe during St Brigid's night, Shrove Tuesday, All Saints' night and many more. In many cases ritual offerings were made to pacify the saints and gain reward or good luck as a consequence.

59 Local Oral Sources, source B. This is well documented in folklore tradition.

60 For further expansion on holy wells, see Raymond Gillespie, 'Popular and unpopular religion' in Kerby Miller and J. S. Donnelly (eds.), *Irish popular culture, 1650–1850* (Dublin, 1998), p. 39.

61 Local Oral Sources, source B.

62 Local Oral Sources, source A.

63 John Curran of Tory Island had his wife's red hair shorn in 1898 because he believed it was the cause of his bad luck. Then he murdered her. He was found unfit to plead.

64 Local Oral Sources, Grace Sweeney tells that in 1918 her young sister was ill and a middle-aged neighbour was also ill. The neighbour's cousin who was famed for his evil powers was watched by a number of neighbours coming across the mountain towards

Grace Sweeney's home. He stopped some distance away where he had a good view of the homes of both patients. He looked for a long time at both homes before nodding his head towards Grace's house. Her sister died that night.

65 Donnchadh Devenney, *Footprints through the Rosses* (Dublin, 1993), pp 36–41.

66 Local Oral Sources, source B.

67 General Register Office, Dublin, marriage registers Glenties, 1895–1906.

68 Esker Archives, p. 81.

69 Local Oral Sources, source B.

70 Heads of households in Meendernasloe in 1901, with 1851 figures in brackets were: Boner 3(2); Boyle 6 (6); Brennan 1 (1); Doogan 3 (2); Doran 1 (1); Duffy 3 (4); Gallagher 3 (4); Harley 3 (3); McBride 5 (6); McGee 2 (2); O'Donnell 8 (7); Roarty 2 (2); Rodgers (Rogers) 12 (14); Sharkey 1 (2); Sweeney 4 (2). Breslan, Ferry, Healy and Russell of 1851 had been replaced by Gordon and Haltam in 1901. (Sources: census of population 1901 and Griffith's Valuation 1851.)

71 General Register Office, Dublin. Glenties district, 1895.

72 NA, Convict Reference Files, (CRF) Misc. Hugh Boyle, 1524/1910, 3/786/5311, Petitions,

73 Local Oral Sources, source F.

74 NA, C.R.F., petition of Hugh Boyle.

75 Eugenia Shanklin, 'Sure what did we ever do but knit' in *Donegal Annual*, 1988, no. 40, pp 40–54.

76 General Register Office, Dublin, Glenties district, 1898.

77 Local oral sources. Source B.

78 NA, CRF, petition of Hugh Boyle. Local Oral Sources, source A says that Conell disapproved of the marriage on two grounds, the youth of the couple and because Mary Harley was carrying on an affair with a tea- salesman who used to visit the area from time to time. However other Local Oral Sources differ on this point. Source B says that the affair with the salesmen took place after her marriage when Hugh was in Scotland and was probably the cause of the row over the

potatoes. I believe this latter version to be the most likely. (This point is further elaborated in footnote 92).

79 NA, Census of population 1901, Annagry DED, no. 55, Meendernasloe no. 15. This census shows that no man in the townland lived on his own. Older men tended to form part of extended families of which there were 15 households out of 59 in the townland.

80 Local Oral Sources. Sources B and F both knew her. Mary Harley is remembered locally as being about 5 ft. 7 in. tall, very thin with very dark hair and a sallow complexion.

81 Local Oral Sources, source B heard this account from a parent who had a close relative living in Meendernasloe not far from Conell Boyle's residence.

82 Transcripts, p. 6.

83 *LS*, 30 Jan. 1897. On 26 Nov. 1897 fire destroyed a cottage in Burtonport. 'The house was occupied by a man named Dan Boyle, his wife and three sons. The father and mother slept in the kitchen. The other members of the family occupied the bedroom. In the kitchen there was a cow, calf, a stack of straw piled in the corner, oats, potatoes, provisions, etc. It was here that the fire originated.'

84 *Census 1841* shows that two thirds of the houses in the Rosses were class 4. Bothóg: local name for mud cabin, generally a class 4 house.

85 Michael Herity (ed.), John O'Donovan, *Ordnance Survey Letters from Donegal 1835* (Dublin, 2000), p. 93. O'Donovan departed from the Rosses on 16 October 1835. At Gweebarra, O'Donovan met a group of women carrying bundles of hand-knit sweaters and gloves on their way to Glenties, eight miles further south. They were 'comely', badly dressed, their faces blackened with peat smoke which was due to their living in 'windowless, smoke filled, mud cabins'. His letters describe a completely isolated area, very heavily populated, with no service of any kind and the people over dependent on the potato as a food source.

86 Local Oral Sources, source B.

87 *DJ,* 9 Dec. 1898, p. 8.

88 Transcripts, pp 25–6.

89 Local Oral Sources, source A states that the house fell three times during its construction. In the local tradition if a house fell during building it was a sign that the house was built on land reserved to the fairies or where the straw on which a dead person had been washed had been abandoned. Such houses were said to have no luck. If a house fell three times it was a sign of impending disaster.

90 Transcripts, pp 25–6.

91 Ibid.

92 Local Oral Sources. Source B heard a parent say that there were commercial travellers who stayed in Húdaí Duffy's pub from time to time and Mary was 'flirting about with them.' Conell may have been hearing these stories and became very bitter about them. However, there is no evidence of this in the court transcripts or in the newspaper accounts.

93 Local Oral Sources. Sources B, C and F agree on this point. Also NA, CRF, Petitions.

94 *Agricultural statistics* 1898, county Donegal, Glenties union, p. 35.

95 C.D.B, Rosses, p. 1.

96 See footnote 70.

97 *LS,* 16 Mar. 1895, p. 4.

98 *LS,* 13 Oct. 1898, p. 7.

99 *LS,* 13 Oct. 1898, p. 7.

100 *LS,* 13 Oct. 1898, p. 7.

101 *LS,* 18 June 1898, p. 7.

102 *LS,* 19 Mar. 1898, p. 7.

103 *LS,* 3 Sept. 1898, p. 7. Letter regarding Gaelic speaking areas of Donegal.

104 *LS,* 3 Sept. 1898, p. 8.

105 'Droch dheoir' was the term given to an evil strain or malevolent trait in a person or family. The identification of such a characteristic would not be welcome in marriage prospects.

106 *DJ,* 12 Dec. 1898, p. 7.

2. A FEARFUL TRAGEDY

1 *DJ,* 5 Sept. 1898, 'The tragedy in County Donegal,' testimony of Margaret Forker.

2 Transcripts, pp 24–30.

3 Transcripts, pp 12–18.

4 See Gearoid O Crualaoich, 'The merry wake' in Chris Curtin and Thomas F. Wilson (eds), *Ireland from below* (Galway, undated). 'A pregnant woman should not attend a wake and should certainly not be present while a corpse is being coffined.' p. 178.

5 Transcripts, pp 6–12.

6 *DJ,* 5 Sept. 1898, 'The Annagry Murder,' Testimony of Hugh Boner.

7 *DJ,* 5 Sept. 1898, 'The Annagry Murder,' Testimony of Mary Boner and Ellen O'Donnell.

8 Transcripts, p. 174.

9 Some papers name him M'Mahon I call him McMacken which is the name in the court transcripts.

10 *DJ,* 5 Sept. 1898, testimony of Acting-Sergeant John McMacken.

11 Transcripts, pp 179–80.

12 Angela Bourke, *The burning of Bridget Cleary* (London, 1999), p. 9.

13 Transcripts, pp 179–80.

14 *DJ,* 9 Dec. 1898, p. 8.

15 *LS,* 3 Sept. 1898, p. 8.

16 *DJ,* 9 Dec. 1898, p. 8.

17 Transcripts, p. 123.

18 Local Oral Sources, source A.

19 *DJ,* 5 Sept. 1898, p. 3.

20 Ibid.

21 Transcripts, p. 180.

22 Transcripts, p. 179.

23 Maurna Crozier, 'Powerful wakes and perfect hospitality' in Curtin and Wilson (eds.), *Ireland from below,* p. 72, 'wake performances are based on the premise that the shared grief subsumes all normal conflicts whether of status, prestige, economic rivalry or personal antagonism.'

24 *DJ,* 9 Dec. 1898, 'The Donegal murder,'.

25 General Register Office. His death certificate recorded that he was a bachelor.

26 Local Oral Sources, source E.

27 *DJ,* 26 Sept. 1898, p. 2.

28 *LS,* 10 Dec. 1898, p. 7.

29 Seán Ó Suilleabháin, *Irish folk custom and belief* (Cork, 1967), p. 53.

30 Ó Suilleabháin, *Irish folk custom and belief,* p. 58. Also Local Oral Sources, source B.

31 Mallacht an bháis' (the curse of death) was greatly feared in a society where ghosts, spirits, superstition and omens were very much part of their lives.

32 There was general denial by all the witnesses throughout the trial that there was any trouble about the crops. But all Local Oral Sources to whom I spoke say that there was serious disagreement and it was the main contention of the prosecution in their opening statements of the trial. This is confirmed in *DJ*, 9 Dec 1898, 'The Donegal murder'.

33 Transcripts, pp 2–15.

34 *DJ*, 5 Sept. 1898, p. 3.

35 Ibid.

36 Ibid.

37 Ibid.

38 Ibid.

39 *DJ*, 26 Sept. 1898, p. 2.

40 Ibid.

41 Local Oral Sources. There is common consensus locally of the event though the red lead aspect is not mentioned in the court transcripts or in the newspapers.

42 Transcripts, p. 176.

43 Transcripts, p. 173.

44 *DJ*, 12 Dec. 1898, p. 7.

45 See O Crualaoich's 'The merry wake,' 'The special "keeners" also cry over the corpse from time to time during the wake. These are old women who are especially good at crying.'

46 Local Oral Sources, Grace Sweeney. This was normal practice in the area until the late 1920s. The new Irish College was built in Ranafast (a townland in the same parish as Annagry) in 1926 to cater for adults, especially teachers. A burial was to take place in Annagry after Sunday mass during that Summer and the curate, Fr Paddy Carr, told the congregation that the students were coming to the cemetery to hear the 'mná caointe' performing and were looking forward to the amusement. He asked that there be no caoineadh or keening. That ended the practice both at the graveside and in the homes in the area. It was one of the defining breaks between the old world and the new.

47 Transcripts, p. 136.

48 Local Oral Sources, source B.

49 See footnote 74.

50 Transcripts, p. 188.

51 Transcripts, pp 131–2.

52 *DJ*, 5 Oct. 1898, p. 8.

53 *DJ*, 5 Oct. 1898, p. 7.

54 *DJ*, 5 Oct. 1898, p. 8.

55 Transcripts, pp 21–37.

56 *DJ*, 16 Sept. 1898, p. 8.

57 Local Oral Sources, source B.

58 *DJ*, 5 Oct. 1898, p. 8.

59 *DJ*, 16 Sept. 1898, p. 8.

60 *LS*, 4 Oct. 1898. 'The Annagry Murder'.

61 *DJ*, 5 Oct. 1898, p. 8.

62 Ibid.

63 Béal druidthe; a closed mouth, a local phrase for non-disclosure of information.

64 Local Oral Sources, source B in particular but this is mentioned by many locally.

65 Local Oral Sources, source B.

66 *DJ*, 5 Oct. 1898, p. 7.

67 *DJ*, 5 Oct. 1898, p. 7.

68 *DJ*, 9 Dec. 1898, 'The Donegal Murder,'.

69 *DJ*, 5 Oct. 1898, p. 8.

70 *DJ*, 9 Dec. 1898, 'The Donegal Murder,'.

71 Ibid.

72 *DJ*, 5 Oct. 1898, p. 8, col. 3.

73 Ó Grianna, *Nuair a bhí mé óg*, pp 114–23 tells of a night of ghost storytelling in Meendernasloe about this time. Local Oral Sources, sources B and F.

74 Ó Crualaoich, 'The merry wake,' 'It is wrong and dangerous to go to or come from a wake alone since the souls of the deceased and of other ancestors are likely to be encountered in the vicinity of the corpse house and there is safety in numbers. Between midnight and daybreak especially, the spirits of the dead and the fairies are likely to be very active about the corpse house.'

75 Ó Crualaoich, 'The merry wake', 'Unnatural deaths result in the dead person being in the fairies.' See also Waldron's *'Maamtrasna,'* p. 154, 'Myles' (Joyce) ghost was to haunt the lives of numerous men and women for years to come.'

76 One of the most feared curses in olden times was to wish a person death without a priest. ('Bás gan sagart ort').

77 Píopa Chondaí: A pipe running under the Annagry to Crolly road.
78 Local Oral Sources, source B.
79 See Lawrence J. Taylor, *Occasions of faith* (Dublin, 1995), pp 73–6, on the theme of 'the returning dead'. 'There are other stories about other spots on the landscape, also powerful, but dangerous. Such places – called *uaigneach*- lonely- are also portals of another world, the world of fairies and /or ghosts.'
80 Local Oral Sources, source B.

3. TWO SCALES OF JUSTICE

1 *Thom's Directory, 1900*. The Right Hon. Sir Peter O'Brien, Bart. (United Kingdom 1891), PC, MA, LLD (TCD) was fourth son of John O'Brien JP of Elm Vale and Ballynalacken Castle, Co. Clare. Born in 1842, he was called to the Bar in 1865, made QC in 1880, crown prosecutor for Dublin 1883, third sergeant-at-law in 1884, solicitor-general for Ireland in 1887 and attorney general for Ireland 1888 – 89 He became lord chief justice of Ireland in 1889. He resided at 41 Merrion Square, Dublin. O'Brien was a Roman Catholic.
2 Waldron, *Maamtrasna*, p. 281. O'Brien's conduct during the prosecution of the Maamtrasna defendants led to a House of Commons debate and accusations that O'Brien had placed the letter C, denoting Catholic, in front of five jurors' names. He was also accused of withholding a document from the defence. Even Gladstone had personally questioned him.
3 Local Oral Sources, source B.
4 Ibid.
5 *DJ*, 9 Dec. 1898, 'The Donegal murder'.
6 The jury was composed of twelve Belfast men.
7 *DJ*, 9 Dec. 1898, p. 7.
8 Partible inheritance and sub-division of land was a common practice in the Annagry area during the second half of the nineteenth century and was a major cause of the continued rise in population there.

9 *DJ*, 9 Dec. 1898, 'The Donegal murder', opening address of attorney-general.
10 *LS*, 10 Dec. 1898, p. 7.
11 Ó Grianna, *Nuair a bhí mé óg*, outlines the problems with learning and understanding English in three chapters, 'an tseanscoil,' 'Lá an easbaig,' and 'an misean.'
12 *DJ*, 12 Dec. 1898, p. 7.
13 *LS*, 10 Dec. 1898, p. 7.
14 Transcripts, p. 9.
15 Transcripts, p. 26.
16 Transcripts, p. 25.
17 Transcripts, p. 30.
18 Transcripts, p. 36.
19 Transcripts, pp 40–86.
20 Transcripts, pp 158–60.
21 Transcripts, pp 161–71.
22 Transcripts, pp 179–81.
23 *LS*, 13 Dec. 1898, p. 8.
24 *DJ*, 12 Dec. 1898, p. 8.
25 *DJ*, 12 Dec. 1898, p. 7.
26 *LS*, 13 Dec. 1898, p. 8.
27 *DJ*, 12 Dec. 1898, p. 8.
28 *LS*, 13 Dec. 1898, p. 8.
29 DJ, 12 Dec. 1898, p. 8, col. 2.
30 Ibid.
31 Local Oral Sources, source B.
32 *DJ*, 12 Dec. 1898, p. 8.
33 Local Oral Sources, source B.
34 Transcripts, information from the governor of Derry gaol on Hugh's transfer form to Maryborough.
35 *LS*, 24 Dec. 1894, p. 8.
36 NA, CRF, James Boyle's letter.
37 NA, CRF, Sir Peter O'Brien's letter.
38 NA, CRF, letter and petition dated 10 Dec. 1898. Forty-eight signatures are appended but there were none from Meendernasloe. Rather than ascribe any base motive to this omission it is more than likely that there was no one in the townland deemed worthy of the status for such a high calling.
39 Michael Cleary was convicted for the murder of his wife, Bridget in the famous Tipperary witch-burning case. See Bourke, *The burning of Bridget Cleary*.
40 Lynchehaun had been sentenced for a brutal murder of a woman in Achill island.
41 A family of five people was wiped out, murdered in their own home on the

night of 17 August 1882 in Maamtrasna, county Galway. Three men, Myles Joyce, Pat Joyce and Pat Casey had been hanged in December 1882 and three more served twenty years in gaol. See Waldron, *Maamtrasna, the murders and the mystery*.

42 Local Oral Sources. The great majority of local people told me this same general story with some minor variations. It is this version of events which is accepted in the area.

43 Local Oral Sources, source B.

44 Local Oral Sources, source B. Bayonne was a favoured emigration destination for Annagry emigrants in the latter half of the nineteenth century.

45 NA, CRF, petition of 1902.

46 NA, CRF, prison petition 1906.

47 Local Oral Sources, source B. See also IFC, Ordnance Survey letters of John O'Donovan from Queen's county, 1838, TSP 109, ms., p. 227, 'The Irish still believe that the stain caused by the blood of a murdered person can never be removed.'

48 Valuation Office, Dublin, Cancellation Books, townland of Meendernasloe, County Donegal.

49 Local Oral Sources, source A.

50 NA, CRF, prison petition 1909.

51 Local Oral Sources, source B.

52 Ibid.

53 Esker Archives, pp 79–81.

54 Esker Archives, p. 81.

55 Local Oral Sources. Two people told me this story in 2000.

56 Local Oral Sources. Source B knew them in Bayonne and is certain that they never had a family.

57 Local Oral Sources, source A.